CW00742274

WREXHAM FOOTBALL CLUB

An A-Z

Dean Hayes

Copyright © Dean P. Hayes, 1998

All Rights Reserved. No part of this publication may be reproduced, stored in a retrieval system, or transmitted in any form or by any means – electronic, mechanical, photocopying, recording, or otherwise – without prior written permission from the publisher.

Published by Sigma Leisure – an imprint of
Sigma Press, 1 South Oak Lane, Wilmslow, Cheshire SK9 6AR, England.

British Library Cataloguing in Publication Data
A CIP record for this book is available from the British Library.

ISBN: 1-85058-640-3

Typesetting and Design by: Sigma Press, Wilmslow, Cheshire.

Printed by: MFP Design & Print

Cover Design: The Agency, Wilmslow

Photographs: David Lovett, *Wrexham Evening Leader*; *The Lancashire Evening Post*; personal collection of Dean P. Hayes.

Acknowledgments: Wrexham Football Club; The British Newspaper Library; The National Library of Wales; Wrexham Library; Harris Library; Chester Record Office; Clwyd Record Offices; The Gwynedd Archives; The Association of Football Statisticians; Wrexham Evening Leader; The Football League Ltd; also the following individuals: Harry Williams; Iain Price; Gareth Jones; Stephen Whittle; Robert Lomas; Ben Hayes; David Lovett; Mike Dean; Fred Williams; Les Evans and Cyril Walker. And to Karen Henderson for the 'X' entry.

Foreword

I was absolutely delighted to be asked to make a contribution to this book about such a wonderful Football Club. This is a friendly, family club who openly encourage the community spirit, the team even let me join in their training sessions, and gave me encouragement and support for my preparation of the London marathon.

I regularly share with the supporters, my family and friends, the ups and downs of 'The Robins'. Along with those dedicated fans, I am very much looking forward to visiting Maine Road, the Britannia Stadium and the Madejski Stadium this season, singing my heart out with 'the red army', and returning home without a voice.

There is a huge reservoir of talent at Wrexham Football Club. The training facilities at Colliers Park and the management structure are unique. The team is professional, dedicated and loyal and there is absolutely no reason why the elusive, but well-deserved promotion shouldn't come soon.

This essential book, a must for every Wrexham supporter, will tell you everything you need to know about The Racecourse and Rush, Goals and Giant killers.

I am proud to be associated with the team, the management and the community, which support Wrexham F.C. and would like to wish them every possible success for the coming season.

COME ON YOU REDS!

Paul Burrell RVM
The Diana Princess of Wales Memorial Fund

ABANDONED MATCHES

An abandoned match may be defined as one which is called off by the referee whilst it is in progress because conditions do not permit it to be completed. Far fewer matches are abandoned in modern times because if there is some doubt about the ability to play the full game, the match is more likely to be postponed.

On 9th April 1927, a crowd of just 952 braved the elements to turn up at the Racecourse Ground for the Third Division (North) game against Lincoln City. With just 19 minutes left, Wrexham were leading 2-0 when the referee abandoned the game after four Lincoln players collapsed because of the cold wet conditions!

Below is a full list of abandoned matches involving Wrexham:

Date	Opponents	Score	Reason
14.11.1896	Chester (H)	2-0	Rain (45 mins)
16.11.1901	Port Vale (H)	1-0	Fog (60 mins)
05.12.1903	Nantwich (H)	4-0	Fog (75 mins)
24.12.1910	Wolves Res (H)	1-1	Broken Crossbar(65 mins)
11.01.1913	Willenhall Swifts(H)	2-1	Waterlogged (48 mins)
22.03.1913	West Brom Res (H)	0-0	Waterlogged (45 mins)
09.04.1927	Lincoln City (H)	2-0	Players Ill (71 mins)
26.12.1933	Tranmere Rovers (H)	1-1	Fog (58 mins)
07.01.1952	Colwyn Bay (A)	0-0	Snowstorm (20 mins)
22.12.1962	Halifax Town (H)	1-1	Fog (30 mins)
16.01.1974	Blaenau Ffestiniog(H)	0-0	Waterlogged (28 mins)
28.03.1979	Newcastle United (A)	1-1	Waterlogged (45 mins)
28.01.1992	Colwyn Bay (H)	0-1	Fog 64 mins)

AGGREGATE SCORE

Wrexham's highest aggregate score in any competition came in the European Cup Winners' Cup competition of 1986-87 against FC Zurrieq of Malta. The Robins won the first leg in Malta 3-0 and then two weeks later won 4-0 at the Racecourse Ground with Steve Massey, who had scored in the first leg, netting two of the goals.

Gareth Davies

The club's highest aggregate defeat is 11-0 when Everton beat them 5-0 at the Racecourse Ground and 6-0 at Goodison in the League Cup of 1990-91.

APPEARANCES

Arfon Griffiths holds the record for the greatest number of appearances in a Wrexham shirt with a total of 721 games to his credit between 1959 and 1979. Including appearances as a substitute, Griffiths played 591 League games, 45 FA Cup games, 31 League Cup games, 46 Welsh Cup games and seven games in the European Cup Winners' Cup. The players with the highest number of appearances are:

Player	League	FA Cup	Lg Cup	Welsh Cup	Others	Total
A. Griffiths	585(6)	45	30(1)	46	7(1)	713(8)
G. Davies	582(7)	40	36	32(1)	14	604(8)
A. Jones	503	40	0	42	0	575
A. McGowan	408	26	8	36	0	478
J. Jones	378(2)	27	24	36	11(2)	476(4)
M. Sutton	355(5)	38(2)	27	27(1)	14	461(8)
M. Evans	368(15)	30	22	29(2)	10	459(17)
A. Fox	350	23	11	30	0	414
E. May	330(4)	24	19	24	9	406(4)
G. Whittle	288(18)	27	18(4)	31	7	371(22)

ARMSTRONG, CHRIS

Newcastle-born Chris Armstrong started his Football League career with Wrexham and made his debut in a 3-0 defeat at Hartlepool United in November 1989. The following season he was the club's leading scorer with 10 league goals as they finished bottom of the Fourth Division, but in August 1991, he joined Millwall for £100,000.

After some impressive performances for the Londoners, he signed for Crystal Palace 13 months later for £1 million. He ended his first season with the Eagles as their top scorer with 15 goals but it was not enough to save them from relegation. The following season he emerged as the club's bright start with eight goals in the opening ten games and ended the campaign as top scorer with 23 league goals.

The 1994-95 season was one of controversy for Armstrong because he was banned for having proved positive in a drugs test. When he returned he was in rich scoring form but at the end of the season he joined Spurs for £4.5 million, the club record fee for an incoming player.

In 1995-96 Armstrong and Shetringham netted 46 goals between them, a total only bettered by Liverpool's Collymore and Fowler. Though he has since suffered with injuries, his goals towards the end of the 1997-98 campaign helped the White Hart Lane club to avoid relegation from the Premiership.

ASHCROFT, BILLY

Known to the fans as 'King Billy', he made his Wrexham debut in a goal-less draw at Reading just two days after his 18th birthday on 3rd October 1970. He established himself in the first team midway through the 1971-72 season and ended the following campaign as the club's leading scorer. Also during that 1972-73 season he played in the club's first match in Europe in a 1-1 draw in Zurich and then scored the winner in the home leg. Over the next two seasons, he was hampered by injuries but in 1975-76 he returned to fitness and was again the Robins' leading scorer. During the club's European Cup Winners' Cup campaign of that season, he was in fine form, netting both goals in a 2-0 win over Stal Rzeszow of Poland and creating a whole host of problems for RSC Anderlecht in the quarter-final second leg in Belgium.

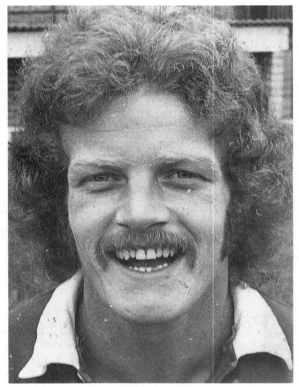

Billy Ashcroft

Forming a good striking partnership with Graham Whittle, he scored 29 League and Cup goals in 54 games during the 1976-77 season, including four in a 6-0 win at Chesterfield.

Unbelievably the club just missed promotion to the Second Division and after just three games of the following season, Ashcroft left the Racecourse Ground to join Middlesbrough for a fee of £120,000 after having scored 96 goals in 272 first team games.

Finding goals hard to come by in the top flight, former Wrexham boss John Neal who was by now 'Boro manager, switched him to centre-half with great success. He had scored 21 goals in 159 league games before leaving to play for Dutch club Twente Enschede.

In 1985 he returned to these shores to play for Tranmere Rovers where he saw out his League career.

ASSOCIATE MEMBERS CUP

The early rounds of this competition, announced by the Football League in December 1983, were run on knockout lines and played on a regional basis, though for some strange reason, the Robins appeared in the Southern section. In the first round, they beat Peterborough United 3-2 with goals from Arkwright, Gregory and Steel before defeating Exeter City 2-0 in front of a Racecourse Ground crowd of just 834. In the quarter-final, Wrexham travelled to Bournemouth but were beaten 2-0.

ATTENDANCE – AVERAGE

Wrexham's average home League attendance's over the last ten years have been as follows:

1988-89	2,239
1989-90	2,386
1990-91	1,888
1991-92	2,647
1992-93	4,987
1993-94	3,961
1994-95	4,071
1995-96	3,705
1996-97	4,112
1997-98	4,109

ATTENDANCE – HIGHEST

The record attendance at the Racecourse Ground is 34,445 for the fourth round FA Cup game with Manchester United on 26th January 1957. Though the Welsh club put up a brave fight, United were by far the superior side and won 5-0. As a matter of interest, the near-35,000 crowd numbered 2,000 more than the entire population of Wrexham at that time!

ATTENDANCE – LOWEST

The lowest attendance for a first team game at the Racecourse Ground is 627 for the visit of Mansfield Town in an Autoglass Trophy preliminary round match on 15th October 1991, which Wrexham won 1-0 through an Andy Preece goal.

AUTOGLASS TROPHY

The Autoglass Trophy replaced the Leyland Daf Cup for the 1991-92 season. The Robins won their first preliminary round match 1-0 at home to Mansfield Town with Andy Preece the goal-scorer. Despite

The Wrexham team, 1982-83

losing their second preliminary round match 2-0 at Peterborough United, the club qualified for the knockout stages and travelled to Bournemouth for the first round match. Two goals from Lee Jones helped Wrexham beat the Cherries 2-1 and so win a place in the Southern Area quarter-final. Again the Robins had to travel, this time to Craven Cottage where goals from Paskin and Phillips gave the club a 2-1 win over Fulham. The Southern Area semi-final saw the Robins paired again with Peterborough United. Sadly for the Welsh club 'Posh' triumphed again, this time 3-1.

In 1992-93, Wrexham beat Crewe Alexandra 3-0 at Gresty Road but then lost 2-0 at home to Stoke City in the preliminary round matches before going out at the next stage.

In 1993-94, Wrexham beat Shrewsbury Town 3-1 with goals from Bennett, Cross and Paskin before travelling to Port Vale where Andy Marriott gave an outstanding display in a goal-less draw. Drawn at home to Colchester United in the next stage of the competition, the Robins had most of the game but lost 1-0 to the Layer Road side.

AUTOWINDSCREEN SHIELD

The Autowindscreen Shield replaced the Autoglass Trophy for the 1994-95 season and in their first match in this newly named competition, the Robins travelled to Gresty Road and gained a creditable 0-0 draw against Crewe Alexandra. Two goals from Gary Bennett then gave Wrexham a 2-0 home win over Mansfield Town and a place in the knockout stages of the competition. Drawn at home to Bradford City, the Robins beat the Yorkshire club 6-1 with Gary Bennett netting a hat-trick. This season, the club were playing in the Northern Section of the Autowindscreen Shield and in the quarter-final travelled to Carlisle United where they were beaten 2-1.

In 1995-96, the Robins drew 2-2 at Mansfield Town before a Karl Connolly strike was enough to beat York City 1-0 and so take the Welsh club into the knockout stages. Again Carlisle United halted the Robins' progress, winning 2-1 at the Racecourse Ground.

The following season the club gained a bye to the second round where they lost 1-0 at home to Crewe Alexandra.

In 1997-98 the Robins again had a bye into the second round but on travelling to Field Mill, lost 1-0 to Mansfield Town.

AWAY MATCHES

Wrexham's best away wins in the Football League have been the 6-0 defeats of Rochdale in 1936-37 and Chesterfield in 1976-77. The club's biggest away win in any competition is 10-0 in a Welsh Cup tie at Welshpool on 26th January 1907. Wrexham's worst defeat away from home is the 9-0 thrashing handed out by Brentford on 15th October 1963, though the club also conceded nine goals in an FA Cup third round tie at Wolverhampton Wanderers on 10th January 1931, when the Molineux club won 9-1. During the 1941-42 Football Regional League North Division, the Robins were beaten 10-3 by Manchester United in a game played at Maine Road because Old Trafford had suffered bomb damage.

AWAY SEASONS

The club's highest number of away wins came in 1961-62 when they won 10 of their 22 matches in winning promotion from the Fourth Division. That season also saw them score a record 40 league goals away from home, a total since equalled in 1970-71.

Wrexham's fewest away wins (one) occurred in seasons 1922-23, 1951-52 and 1982-83.

B

BAMFORD, TOMMY

Born in Port Talbot, Tommy Bamford worked in the Cardiff Docks and played for their team as well as Bridgend Town before joining Wrexham towards the end of the 1928-29 season. He played in the last seven matches of that campaign and scored six goals. In 1929-30 he was the club's top scorer with 25 goals in 37 league games including four in an 8-0 home win over Rochdale. The following season he netted 34 goals in 35 league appearances including another haul of four in a 6-1 defeat of Accrington Stanley at the Racecourse Ground. He topped the charts again in 1931-32 with 30 goals in 35 league games and after hat-tricks against Doncaster Rovers (Home 4-2) and

Chester (Away 5-2) he netted four goals for the third time in his career in a 5-1 home win over Walsall.

This form led to him winning the first of five full international caps for his country when he scored against Scotland in a 1-1 draw at Hampden Park in October 1931.

In 1932-33 when the club finished runners-up in the Third Division (North), Bamford scored 31 goals in 40 league games, including four hat-tricks against Accrington Stanley (Away 3-5), Barnsley (Away 3-5), Gateshead (Home 5-1) and Rotherham United (Home 5-1).

The following season he scored a club record 44 goals in 41 league appearances including five goals in the 8-1 home win over Carlisle United and all four in a 4-1 win at Doncaster Rovers. After scoring 207 goals in 245 first team games, he signed for Manchester United along with team-mate William Bryant.

The Old Trafford club signed him shortly after they had paid a visit to Wrexham to play a match in aid of the Gresford Colliery disaster fund. Though he was not so quite prolific for United, he showed his consistency by finishing as their leading marksman in two successive seasons.

He returned to South Wales to play for Swansea Town in 1938 and continued his career for them in the early part of the war.

BANNAN, TOMMY

Tommy Bannan played his early football in his native Scotland with Airdrie before moving south to join Wrexham in the summer of 1951. He scored on his debut at Chester in the opening match of the 1951-52 season and at Barrow five days later, but both matches ended in defeat for the Robins.

In 1952-53 he was the club's leading scorer with 18 league goals and the following season netted his first hat-trick for the club in an 8-0 home win over Workington. At the end of the 1954-55 season after which he had scored 73 goals in 182 games he left the Racecourse Ground to join Lincoln City for a fee of £1,000. Bannan spent two seasons at Sincil Bank, where he scored 19 goals in 67 league appearances. He returned to Wrexham for a second spell in the summer of 1957 and had a very successful Welsh Cup campaign, scoring in every round. He hit a hat-trick in a 7-0 win over Flint Town and the club's second goal in the 2-1 win in the final replay. In 1958-59 he was again the club's top scorer but at the end of the season he was transferred to Barrow where he ended his league career.

BARNES, KEN

As an amateur with non-League Stafford Rangers, his performances attracted the attentions of Birmingham City, West Bromwich Albion and Sheffield Wednesday but it was Manchester City who snapped him up. He played in 283 first team games for City, scoring 19 goals. Described by Denis Law as 'the finest uncapped wing-half who ever played English football' he gained both FA Cup winners' and runners-up medals and also represented the Football League.

In May 1961, he joined Wrexham as player-manager, replacing Billy Morris and made his debut in a 1-0 win at Millwall on the opening day of the 1961-62 season. By the end of that campaign he had led the Robins to promotion from the Fourth Division, though in 1963-64 they were relegated after two seasons in the higher grade. Midway through the following season, Chester beat the Robins 6-1 and Barnes lost his job to Billy Morris, the man he replaced when he arrived at the Racecourse Ground.

Barnes had scored 24 goals in 132 League games for Wrexham in his role as player-manager. On leaving the Welsh club, he moved into non-League football as player-manager of Witton Albion before managing Bangor City. He later returned to Maine Road as trainer-coach before becoming the chief scout.

BAYNES, JACK

Jack Baynes began his Football League career with Rotherham County and then coached at non-League Mansfield Town, taking them to two Midland League championships in his time at Field Mill. In 1925 he joined Nottingham Forest but during his four years at the City Ground, it was largely an undistinguished period of their history.

In October 1929, Baynes was appointed Wrexham's second manager, succeeding Charlie Hewitt who had left the Racecourse Ground in 1926. During the three years between the appointments, the team had been selected by the directors. After a season of struggle, the Robins finished fourth in 1930-31 and won the Welsh Cup beating Shrewsbury Town 7-0 in the final. Baynes looked to have produced a side capable of making the Second Division but in September 1931, he was admitted to Chester Royal Infirmary for 'operative treatment' on a cancer and although he was allowed home, three months later, he suffered a relapse and died, aged only 43.

BENNETT, GARY

Gary Bennett joined Wigan Athletic from Kirby Town in October 1984, and though he couldn't win a regular first team place, he was a member of the Latics' side that beat Brentford 3-1 at Wembley in the final of the Freight Rover Trophy in 1985. At the end of that season he joined Chester City on a free transfer and in 155 games for the then Sealand Road club, scored 47 goals before leaving to play for Southend United. He didn't really settle at Roots Hall and after just over a year he returned to play for Chester.

In August 1992, Bennett joined Wrexham and after scoring 16 goals in 35 league games that season, finished second in the Division Two scoring charts with 36 League and Cup goals, including a hat-trick in a 3-0 home win over Hull City. In 1994-95 Bennett topped the divisional scoring charts with 39 goals, netting hat-tricks in the wins over Leyton Orient and Wycombe Wanderers both of which ended in 4-1 wins for the Robins.

At the end of that season he joined Tranmere Rovers for a fee of £300,000 but after a disappointing season at Prenton Park he became Preston North End's record signing when they paid £200,000 for his services.

During his time at Deepdale he was kept out of first team action with a series of injuries including a shin fracture. When he did return he netted two goals in the 3-0 derby win over Blackpool before returning to the Racecourse Ground for £100,000.

He took his tally of goals for the Robins to 103 in 170 games before leaving to join Chester for a third time.

Gary Bennett

BEST START

Wrexham were unbeaten for the first 10 games of the 1928-29 season when they won seven and drew three of their fixtures before losing 6-2 at Stockport County.

BIGGEST DEFEATS

The club's biggest defeat in the Football League occurred on 15th October 1963, when they were hammered 9-0 by Brentford at Griffin Park. The club's record defeat in the FA Cup was inflicted upon them on 10th January 1931, when Wolverhampton Wanderers won the third round tie at Molineux 9-1.

BIGGEST WINS

The club's biggest win in the Football League occurred on 3rd March 1962, when Hartlepool United were beaten 10-1 in a Fourth Division encounter with Wrexham players, Wyn Davies, Roy Ambler and Ron Barnes all scoring hat-tricks.

When Wrexham entertained New Brighton in the first round of the Football League Northern Section Cup on 3rd January 1934, they won 11-1 with Tommy Bamford scoring five of the goals and William Bryant a hat-trick.

BIRMINGHAM AND DISTRICT LEAGUE

The club's first season in the Birmingham and District League was 1905-06 when despite playing the reserve teams of Aston Villa, Birmingham, Stoke, West Bromwich Albion and Wolverhampton Wanderers, Wrexham finished the season in a very creditable sixth place.

In 1907-08 the club experienced the highs and lows of the game. On 14th September 1907, they lost 8-1 to West Bromwich Albion Reserves at The Hawthorns to suffer their heaviest defeat in the League so far, but on 2nd November 1907, they beat the eventual champions, Aston Villa, 2-1 at Villa Park. The following season the club gained their biggest win in the League so far when they beat Burton United 9-0.

During the 1912-13 season, the club's eighth in the competition, they were registered as a Limited Company, which meant the beginning of professional football at Wrexham.

During the 1914-15 season in which Wrexham finished sixth, they beat Birmingham Reserves 6-2 at the Racecourse Ground in a Christmas Day fixture. In the first peacetime season of 1919-20, Wrexham finished in third place, their best-ever position in the Birmingham and District League. The following season was to be the club's last before they became founder members of the Third Division (North). In fact, at one stage it looked as though they would win the championship but had to settle for third place, four points adrift of champions Wellington Town, after failing to win any of their last four games.

BLACKBURN, ERNEST

After playing League football for Aston Villa and Bradford City, Ernest Blackburn joined Accrington Stanley as trainer in the summer of 1924, becoming secretary-manager at Peel Park a few months later. At Accrington he had to work under the burden of financial problems and though he had charge of the day-to-day running of the club, the directors picked the team.

In January 1932, he was appointed as Wrexham manager and in his first season at the Racecourse Ground, the club came very close to promotion, finishing as runners-up to Hull City. He stayed at Wrexham until January 1937, when he was offered the manager's job at Boothferry Park. He helped reduce the Yorkshire club's debts and in 1938, the Tigers just missed out on promotion to Division Two. After keeping the club going through the way years, Blackburn was surprisingly not retained at the end of the hostilities and became the first manager to lose his job after the war.

He later became secretary-manager of Tranmere Rovers where he produced successful and entertaining sides before in 1955 relinquishing team duties to concentrate on administration.

BLEW, HORACE

One of Wrexham's best pre-war footballers, Horace Blew, later an alderman and mayor of Wrexham, played his first match for the club in a 5-2 away win against Druids in a Combination League fixture in September 1897.

Though he had a number of offers to play League football, he only appeared in two games, one for Manchester United and one for Manchester City. Following his appearance for United in a match against

Chelsea in April 1906, which they drew 1-1, a special gold medal was struck for him to commemorate the Old Trafford club's promotion.

With Wrexham, Blew won four Combination League championship medals and appeared in six Welsh Cup finals, gaining three winners' medals in 1903, 1905 and 1909.

He represented Wales on 22 occasions, the most notable being against England at Ninian Park in 1906 when after his fellow fullback A.T. Jones of Nottingham Forest went off injured, he played a lone role against the English forwards for an hour.

Just before he ended his playing days, Wrexham tried to arrange a benefit match for Blew in recognition for his loyal service, but the Welsh FA had other ideas and refuted the idea on the grounds of his amateur status. Blew as he had before, turned professional and then returned to his amateur status after receiving just reward for his 14 years at the Racecourse Ground.

Blew played the last of his 287 games for his home-town club in March 1911, after which he became a club director.

BROTHERS

There have been a number of instances of brothers playing for Wrexham. Perhaps the most famous were the Spruce brothers.

George was the elder brother of Phil Spruce and after making his debut in a 2-2 draw at home to Hartlepool United on 6th November 1948, he went on to appear in 156 League and Cup games for the club before joining Barnsley. At Oakwell, he helped the Yorkshire club win promotion to the Second Division before ending his league career with his home-town club Chester.

Phil Spruce made his League debut for Wrexham against his home-town club on the opening day of the 1951-52 season, which was George's last at the Racecourse Ground. Though he went on to play in 23 League games, the two brothers never played in the same Wrexham side.

BURGON, ARCHIE

Initially a centre-forward, Archie Burgon scored twice in a trial match for Notts. County but he was not offered terms and joined Newark Town. He performed so well for Newark at either centre-forward or outside-left that County decided they might have made a mistake and offered him a position on the staff. However, he was unable to make the step up to League level and was allowed to join Midland League side Grantham Town. His performances led to him being signed by Tottenham Hotspur but after just nine months at White Hart Lane he joined Wrexham.

He made his League debut for the Robins in a 1-1 draw at York City in November 1935, and after being switched to outside-left became a virtual ever-present in the Wrexham side for the next four seasons. In 1936-37 he scored 20 goals in 42 League and Cup outings including a hat-trick in a 5-0 home win over Crewe Alexandra.

At the end of the 1938-39 season and after scoring 39 goals in 147 League and Cup games he returned to non-League football before ending his playing career during the Second World War.

Steve Buxton

BUXTON, STEVE

A Welsh Schoolboy international, Steve Buxton played his first game for the Robins as a substitute in a 2-1 defeat at Sheffield Wednesday on the final day of the Third Division championship-winning season of 1977-78. Though he didn't establish himself as a first team regular until 1982-83 he contributed some vital goals during the club's four seasons of Second Division football.

In 1982-83 he scored 13 goals in 49 first team appearances, the best return of his career, but at the end of the following season he left the Racecourse Ground to play in Sweden. When he returned he joined Stockport County but only made 22 first team appearances for the Hatters before entering non-League football with Altrincham.

After the Wrexham squad was decimated by injuries, he was offered another contract and continued to play for the club until the end of the 1989-90 season. Buxton scored 66 goals in 299 first team appearances before joining Telford United along with team-mate Neil Salathiel.

CAPACITY

The total capacity of the Racecourse Ground in 1997-98 was 9,200.

CAPTAINS

Among the many players who have captained the club are Arthur Lea, who only had one arm and was the Wrexham skipper when they won the Welsh Cup for the first time, beating Chirk 2-1 at Oswestry on 3rd April 1893.

Ted Robinson captained Wrexham to four Combination League championships and eight Welsh Cup Finals of which the club won three.

Eddie May captained the Wrexham side for most of his eight seasons at the Racecourse Ground. He skippered the Robins in two European campaigns and in 1974 led the club to the sixth round of the FA

Cup for the first time in their history. May was also the captain when Wrexham won promotion to the Third Division in 1969-70.

CARRODUS, FRANK

Starting his career with his home-town club, Altrincham, Frank Carrodus moved into League football in November 1969, with Manchester City. He appeared in 49 first team games for the Maine Road club before joining Aston Villa in the summer of 1974.

Frank Carrodus

In his first season with the Villa Park side he helped them win promotion to the First Division and picked up a League Cup winners' medal. after Villa had beaten Norwich City 1-0 at Wembley. Carrodus won a second League Cup winners' medal in 1977 as Villa defeated Everton over three matches. He had played in 197 League and Cup games for Villa before moving to Wrexham in December 1979.

He made his debut for the Robins in a 3-1 home win over Luton Town and over the next three seasons was a virtual ever-present in the Wrexham side. He left the Racecourse Ground in the summer of 1982 after the club had been relegated to the Third Division, having appeared in 117 League and Cup games.

Having joined Birmingham City, he made just eight appearances in 1982-83 and in October 1983, moved to Bury. When he left Gigg Lane he played non-League football for Runcorn and Witton Albion before leaving the game.

CARTWRIGHT, LES

Midfielder Les Cartwright began his League career as a winger with Coventry City and though he was to spend eight years at Highfield Road, he only made 68 League appearances, scoring four goals. After being capped by Wales at Under-23 level, the Aberdare-born player won the first of seven full caps when he played against England in 1974.

He joined Wrexham in the summer of 1977 for a fee of £40,000 and made his debut in a 1-1 home draw against Port Vale in the third match of the 1977-78 season. He went on to score four goals in 41

Les Cartwright

League appearances that campaign as the Welsh club won the Third Division championship. He also won a Welsh Cup winners' medal, scoring in the 2-1 first leg win at Bangor City. Cartwright also played his part as the club reached the sixth round of the FA Cup, scoring in the 4-1 fourth round replay win over Newcastle United.

Sadly injuries limited his appearances in the Second Division and in March 1982, after scoring 14 goals in 154 first team games he moved to Cambridge United where he ended his League career.

Wayne Cegielski

CEGIELSKI, WAYNE

A Welsh Youth international, central defender Wayne Cegielski began his career with Tottenham Hotspur where he understudied Welsh international Mike England. Unable to break into the first team at White Hart Lane, he joined Northampton Town on loan, where he made his League debut. Though the Cobblers offered him the chance of regular first team football, he turned them down and went to play for West German club VfB Stuttgart and later FC Schalke 04. In the summer of

1976 he went to the United States to play for Seattle Sounders but after asking Wrexham for a trial, he was signed by John Neal and made his debut in a 2-0 defeat at Mansfield Town on 18th December 1976.

Within weeks of his arrival at the Racecourse Ground, he won Welsh Under-21 honours but in his first four seasons with the club, he struggled to hold down a regular first team spot. By 1980-81 he had established himself as the club's first-choice centre-half but was released after 165 appearances following the Robins' relegation in 1982.

Cegielski then joined Port Vale where he was a regular in the club's 1982-83 Fourth Division promotion team and was voted Player of the Year. He went on to play in 102 first team games before moving on to Blackpool on a free transfer in March 1985. He later played for Hereford United, Worcester City and Northwich Victoria.

CENTURIES

There are only two instances of individual players who have scored 100 or more League goals for Wrexham. Tommy Bamford is the greatest goal-scorer with 174 strikes in his Wrexham career (1929-1934). The other centurion is Arfon Griffiths who netted 120 League goals for the Robins.

Only three players have made 100 or more consecutive League appearances immediately following their Wrexham debut. They are Andy Marriott (143), Bobby Shinton (122) and Billy Tunnicliffe (115).

Goalkeeper Brian Lloyd holds the record for the most consecutive League appearances with 248. Other players to have made 100 or more consecutive League appearances during their careers are Alf Jones (201), Alan Fox (163), Alf Jones again!(138), Gareth Davies (135) and Brian Tinnion (122).

CHAMPIONSHIPS

Wrexham have only won one divisional championship. In 1977-78 the Robins won the Third Division championship when they finished three points ahead of their nearest rivals, Cambridge United. The season started badly for the Welsh side, losing one and drawing three of their first four matches. However, they soon strung together an un-

Third Division championship celebration

beaten run of 13 matches of which ten were won. Later in the season, the club won seven consecutive League matches including beating Tranmere Rovers 6-1. Promotion was clinched on 22nd April 1978, when Rotherham United were beaten 7-1 and the championship won on 1st May 1978, when a goal-less draw at home to Peterborough United ensured the title came to the Racecourse Ground.

CHARLES, STEVE

Sheffield-born Steve Charles turned down an apprenticeship with Sheffield Wednesday to continue his education despite being on the Hillsborough club's books since the age of 14. Even when he had completed his schooling he turned down the offer of a full-time contract to attend Sheffield University where he studied for a degree in Mathematics. It was only after graduating that he turned his attentions to football and after a soccer scholarship in America, he signed for Sheffield United in January 1980.

In five seasons at Bramall Lane, Charles played in 148 first team games before joining Wrexham for a fee of £10,000 in November 1984.

On his debut he scored Wrexham's goal in a 1-1 home draw against Hartlepool United and over the next three seasons, rarely missed a game. In 1985-86 he was the club's leading scorer with 21 League goals after having scored in each of Wrexham's first six league games. Also that season, he won a Welsh Cup winners' medal after Kidderminster Harriers were beaten after a replay. He captained the side during their 1986-87 European Cup Winners' Cup campaign and scored the opening goal in the 3-0 win in Malta over FC Zurrieq.

At the end of that season he joined Mansfield Town and went on to play in 278 first team games for the Field Mill club before ending his playing days with Scarborough where he played in the 600th League match of his career.

CHESTER

Main rivals Chester visited the Racecourse Ground for the first time in a League match on 13th September 1890. A crowd of just over 500 saw Wrexham go down 1-0. The first Football League meeting between the two clubs was at the Racecourse Ground on 2nd September 1931. This time a crowd of 18,750 saw the game end 1-1 with Tommy Bamford netting for the Robins. In the return at Sealand Road Bamford scored a hat-trick as Wrexham won 5-2. Chester gained their revenge in 1934-35 with a 6-2 win over Wrexham at Sealand Road.

On Boxing Day 1936 the game against Chester at the Racecourse Ground set a record that still stands today when a crowd of 29,261 watched the visitors win 2-1 with Archie Burgon netting for Wrexham. The attendance is still the record for a League game at the Racecourse Ground.

The wartime fixtures between the clubs threw up some high scoring fixtures with Chester winning 7-2 in 1942-43 and Wrexham 8-4 in 1943-44.

Billy Tunnicliffe scored all three goals, two of them from the penalty-spot in Wrexham's 3-2 win on 26th September 1951, whilst the Robins biggest League win in this fixture came on 25th April 1953, when Chester were beaten 7-0.

The 1997-98 team line-up

CLEAN SHEET

This is the colloquial expression to describe a goalkeeper's perform-ance when he does not concede a goal. Brian Lloyd in 1973-74 had 19 clean sheets in 46 League appearances plus another seven in Cup competitions.

COMBINATION LEAGUE

Wrexham's first game in the Combination League took place on 6th September 1890, when they lost 5-1 at Gorton Villa, with their goal being scored by Arthur Lea, a Welsh international who only had one arm. The following week, Wrexham entertained Chester for the first-ever League meeting between the sides and lost 1-0. In fact, Wrexham did not win until 27th December, when William Turner scored all the goals in a 4-2 home win over Burton Swifts in what was their eighth match. They ended the season in eight place and over the next three seasons, finished sixth, eight and eighth respectively before with-drawing from the Combination due to increased expenditure.

After two seasons in the Welsh League, Wrexham rejoined the Combination League for the 1896-97 season and finished sixth out of ten teams. In 1897-98, the League was extended to 14 teams and Wrexham enjoyed their best season to date, finishing third. After fin-ishing fifth in 1898-99 the club were runners-up in 1899-1900. The following season saw Wrexham finally win the Combination League with a 1-0 home win over Tranmere Rovers giving them the title from their closest rivals Rhyl.

In 1901-02 Wrexham retained the title, finishing eight points clear of runners-up Port Vale reserves. At the Racecourse Ground they won 12 and drew one of their home matches with their best win being the 9-0 hammering of Bangor City. In 1902-03 Wrexham won the title for a third year in a row and inflicted 9-0 defeats on Newton-le-Willows and Bangor City for the second year in succession. The following sea-son saw Wrexham lose their first home game in the Combination for six years when they went down 1-0 to Tranmere Rovers. In 1904-05 Wrexham won the title for the fourth time in five years and in the pro-cess won all 13 home games. It was to be their last season in the Com-bination after being finally accepted in the Birmingham and District League.

COMSTIVE, PAUL

First signing as a professional for Blackburn Rovers, he struggled to make an impact at Ewood Park and experienced only a brief taste of first team action. After a loan spell at Rochdale in 1982 where he scored his first League goal on his debut, he joined Wigan Athletic on a free transfer in August 1983, operating as the Latics' left-back.

In November 1984, he was transferred to Wrexham for £3,000 and again scored on his debut in a 2-1 home defeat by Southend United. He picked up a Welsh Cup winners' medal in 1986 and then in 1986-87 experienced his first taste of European football. At the end of that season he left the Racecourse Ground to join Burnley for a fee of £8,000.

Moved into midfield, he scored some crucial goals including two in the 1987-88 momentous Sherpa Van Trophy campaign. It was Comstive who twice hit the woodwork with headers in the Wembley final against Wolverhampton Wanderers.

In September 1989, he joined Bolton Wanderers for £37,000 and helped them come close to promotion from Division Three in two successive seasons. After losing his place he was transferred to Chester, ending his League career when he was released from the Deva Stadium in the summer of 1993.

He then spent two successful seasons with Southport before joining Morecambe.

CONNOLLY, KARL

Karl Connolly arrived at the Racecourse Ground after being spotted playing for Napoli in the Liverpool Sunday League. He made his debut for Wrexham in a 1-0 home defeat at the hands of Hereford United on the opening day of the 1991-92 season.

Since his debut, Connolly has been a virtual ever-present in the Wrexham side and in 1995-96 after moving from his position wide on the left to that of central striker, he responded by being the club's leading scorer with 18 goals, including a hat-trick in a 4-3 home win over Swindon Town. In fact, his form led to him winning a place in the PFA award-winning Second Division team.

One of the most popular players at the club, he is particularly dangerous at set pieces in and around the box.

In 1996-97, a loss of form persuaded the Prescot-born forward to ask for a transfer. Though a number of clubs showed an interest in him, none of them made an offer. Thankfully, he had a change of heart and in 1997-98 took his goals tally for the club to 86 in 348 games including netting a hat-trick in a 5-2 win at Luton Town on 20th September 1997.

Karl Connolly

CONSECUTIVE HOME GAMES

Wrexham played an intense sequence of six home games in succession in 35 days (10th March – 14th April 1979). They won three – Blackburn Rovers (2-1), Oldham Athletic (2-0) and Preston North End (2-1) – drew two, Fulham (1-1) and Charlton Athletic (1-1) – and lost one, Burnley (0-1).

CONSECUTIVE SCORING – LONGEST SEQUENCE

Tommy Bamford and Kevin Russell share the club record for consecutive scoring when they were on target in nine consecutive league games. Bamford's first came in a 2-2 home draw against Tranmere Rovers on 7th February 1931, and ended with two goals in a 3-2 win at Barrow on 3rd April 1931. Kevin Russell's first goal came on 19th March 1988, as the Robins won 2-0 at Scarborough and ended with a goal in the 2-1 win at Rochdale on 2nd May 1988.

COTTON, BILL

Signed from Garston FC in the summer of 1921, Bill Cotton lined up at centre-forward in the club's first game in the Football League, a 2-0 defeat at home to Hartlepool United. On 5th November 1921, he scored a hat-trick as Wrexham beat Chesterfield 6-1 just being pipped in the race to be the scorer of the club's first hat-trick by Ted Regan who netted the other three goals in that match. The following season he was the club's leading scorer with 12 goals in 31 games and again in 1923-24 with 14 goals in 31 outings, including a hat-trick in a 4-0 home win over Ashington on the opening day of the season.

He played his last match for the club in a goal-less home draw on the final day of the 1923-24 season just two days after he'd scored the winning goal in the Welsh Cup Final victory over Merthyr Tydfil.

Cotton had scored 47 goals in 106 games for Wrexham when he was allowed to leave the Racecourse Ground to play for Kettering Town. He later returned to the Football League with Port Vale before having spells with Halifax Town and Crewe Alexandra.

COWELL, ARTHUR

He began his League career with his home-town club Blackburn Rovers where with Bob Compton, he formed one of the best full-back partnerships in the club's history. Though Compton was capped many times by England, Cowell played only once, against Ireland in Belfast in February 1910. He helped the Ewood Park club to two titles and made a total of 306 League and Cup appearances for Blackburn. Sadly the last few years of his career were marred first by the war and then by injury.

Cowell became Rovers' trainer, a position he held until the summer of 1937 when he was appointed Wrexham's manager, following James Logan's resignation. After only seven matches of the 1938-39 season, he had a disagreement with the Wrexham board and resigned after the 1-0 home win over Rochdale.

CROWD TROUBLE

However unwelcome, crowd disturbances are far from a modern phenomenon at major football matches.

Behaviour at the Racecourse Ground has usually been of a high standard and though Wrexham supporters are well renowned for voicing their opinions at suspect referees, the occasions when their demonstrations boil over beyond the verbal are very rare indeed. However, such an occasion did take place on 1st December 1883, when Wrexham played Oswestry in the second round of the FA Cup. The match which was played at the Racecourse Ground ended in a 4-3 win for Oswestry but the Shropshire club's winning goal was disputed by both Wrexham players and supporters. On the final whistle, the referee had to be escorted from the field by two policemen with the 'Wrexham mob hooting him in a violent and disgraceful manner'.

When Wrexham played Druids at the Racecourse Ground in the Denbighshire and Flintshire Charity Cup Final of 1898-99, Druids, who were trailing 3-1 had a goal disallowed for a foul on the goalkeeper. A number of the Druids supporters rushed on to the field of play and one of them attacked the referee. The game which still had almost ten minutes left to play was brought to an abrupt end and the result allowed to stand.

CUNNINGTON, SHAUN

Shaun Cunnington was just 16 years 338 days old when he made his debut for Wrexham in a 4-0 defeat at Bristol Rovers on 18th December 1982, after former Pirates' player Phil Bater was injured. By the start of the 1983-84 season he had established himself as the club's first-choice left-back and over the next five seasons missed very few games. He was ever-present in 1986-87 when he and Barry Horne were the only two players to play in all of the club's 62 competitive games.

He had played in 269 first team games for the Robins when in February 1988, Grimsby Town paid £50,000 for his services.

In 1989-90 he won a Fourth Division championship medal with the Mariners before helping them win promotion to the Second Division the following season. He had played in 213 first team games for the Blundell Park club when Sunderland splashed out £650,000 in the summer of 1992 to take him to Roker Park. He played in 65 games for the Wearsiders before West Bromwich Albion paid £220,000 for him prior to the start of the 1995-96 season. Knee and ankle injuries ruined his stay at The Hawthorns and in March 1997, he joined Notts. County. Unable to prevent their relegation he was instrumental in the club's promotion to the Second Division in 1997-98.

DAVIES, BILL

Wrexham-born centre-forward Bill 'Tinker' Davies began his footballing career with his home-town club, making his debut in a 3-0 home win over Tranmere Rovers in December 1902. That season, he helped Wrexham win the Combination League Championship, scoring six goals in 13 games including his first hat-trick for the club in a 5-1 home win over Middlewich Rangers. In the Welsh Cup of 1902-03 he netted five goals in a 9-0 win over the Royal Welsh Warehouse and a hat-trick in the 4-0 defeat of Wellington Town before scoring two goals in the 8-0 final victory over Aberamon.

The following season he won the first of two Welsh caps whilst with Wrexham when he played against Ireland but it was 1904-05, the club's last season in the Combination League that was to be Davies' best and also last season with the club. That term, Wrexham carried off four trophies including the Combination League Championship and Welsh Cup again. In the Combination, Davies scored 21 goals in 21 games including another hat-trick in the 7-0 defeat of

Chirk and ended the season with 36 goals in 32 games in all competitions.

At the end of that season he joined Blackburn Rovers where he added nine more caps to his collection and won a Football League Championship medal in 1911-12, his last season at Ewood Park.

DAVIES, DAI

Born in the South Wales mining village of Ammanford, goalkeeper Dai Davies played local football before joining Swansea Town. He had only played in nine league games for the Vetch Field club and was never on the losing side, when in December 1970, he joined Everton for £20,000.

After spending virtually four seasons in the shadow of Gordon West and his understudy David Lawson, Davies went back to the Swans on loan. He returned to Goodison and went on to appear in 94 League and Cup games before leaving to join Wrexham in September

Dai Davies

1977, for £8,000. Whilst with Everton he gained the first of 52 Welsh caps when he played in Wales' 2-1 win over Hungary in Budapest.

In his first season at the Racecourse Ground, Wrexham suffered the lowest number of defeats in their history as they won the Third Division championship. In 1978-79 the Wrexham 'keeper helped establish the club's best-ever defensive record of only 42 goals conceded. The Robins won the Welsh Cup and qualified for Europe.

At the end of the 1980-81 season he returned to Swansea before becoming player-coach of Tranmere Rovers in the summer of 1983. A year later, he retired from the game but in 1985, Bangor City asked him to play in Europe and the following season he turned out in Wrexham's Welsh Cup campaign, winning a medal after Kidderminster Harriers were beaten in the final.

DAVIES, GARETH

After some impressive performances in the Welsh League for both Llandudno and Colwyn Bay, Gareth Davies joined Wrexham and made his debut in a 2-0 home defeat by Bradford City in February 1968. However, it was the following season when Davies established himself as a regular in the Wrexham side and scored his first league goal in a 1-1 draw at Brentford. In 1969-70 he missed just one game as the Robins were promoted from the Fourth Division as runners-up to

Gareth Davies

Chesterfield. In fact, Davies missed very few games over the next 14 seasons, being ever-present in 1976-77 and 1977-78 and playing in 135 consecutive league matches. In this latter season, Wrexham won the Third Division championship and it was his performances during this campaign that led to him winning full international honours, his first cap being against Iran in 1978. The 1977-78 season also saw Third Division Wrexham reach the quarter-finals of both the FA and League Cups and Davies was outstanding in both runs.

Davies won three Welsh Cup winners' medals and shares the record with Mel Sutton of having played in the most European matches for the club – 14 – his only goal in the Cup Winners' Cup coming in the 2-1 home win over Swedish side Djurgardens IF in the opening match of the 1975-76 competition.

He played in 612 first team games for the Robins, second only to Arfon Griffiths before injury forced his retirement at the end of the 1982-83 season.

DAVIES, LLEW

Llew Davies made his Wrexham debut in the final game of the 1900-01 Combination League when Bangor City were beaten 4-2. Over the next two seasons, he was a virtual ever-present as Wrexham won the Combination Championship in successive years. He then had a season with the Druids and helped them reach the final of the Welsh Cup before returning to play for Wrexham. In that 1904-05 season, Davies helped the Robins to win yet another Combination Championship and the Welsh Cup and made his Football League debut for West Bromwich Albion.

In 1907 he won the first of 13 Welsh caps, four during his Wrexham career, when he played against Ireland. In 1901 he left the Racecourse Ground to play for Everton but having failed to make the grade at Goodison Park he joined St Helens.

In November 1911, he returned to Wrexham for a third spell, winning his sixth Welsh Cup winners' medal. Though the First World War interrupted his career he continued to play for Wrexham after the hostilities, playing the last of his 379 first team games at Worcester City in October 1919, in a Birmingham and District League game.

DAVIES, WYN

Born in Caernarfon, Wyn Davies had a spell with Llanberis before joining his home-town club. From there he went into the League with Wrexham and made a goal-scoring debut in a 3-1 home win over Exeter City on the opening day of the 1960-61 season. He went on to score 26 goals in 67 first team games including a hat-trick in his last appearance in a Wrexham shirt as Hartlepool United were beaten 10-1.

He joined Bolton Wanderers in a transfer deal worth £20,000 cash plus Ernie Phythian, who was reportedly valued at £10,000. The big Welshman was quickly installed into the Number nine shirt and except for periods of injury, he was a Bolton regular for four and a half years. In 1964 he won the first of 34 Welsh caps and because of his outstanding performances for the Wanderers, his name became linked with almost every First Division club and in October 1966, Newcastle United paid £80,000 for him.

Davies was a member of the Magpies' 1969 In-

Wyn Davies

ter Cities Fairs Cup-winning team but in August 1971, he returned to the north-west with Manchester City. He moved to Old Trafford and had spells at Blackpool, Crystal Palace and Stockport County before ending his League career at Crewe Alexandra in 1977.

He then spent some time in South Africa playing for Arcadia Shepherds FC before returning to England to play non-League football.

DAVIS, FRED

Wing-half Fred Davis began his Football League career with Reading after he had been spotted playing for Bloxwich Strollers near his home-town of Walsall. During his two and a half years at Elm Park he made 62 league appearances but was released at the end of the 1954-55 season.

Though a number of clubs were after his signature, Davis opted for Wrexham and made his league debut for the Robins in a 3-1 win at York City on the opening day of the 1955-56 season. Over the next six seasons he hardly missed a match and was ever-present in 1960-61, his last season at the Racecourse Ground. During his time with the Robins he won Welsh Cup winners' medals in 1958 and 1960 and helped the club qualify for the Third Division in 1957-58.

His departure from the Racecourse Ground after 265 first team games coincided with the appointment of Ken Barnes as player-manager.

DEBENHAMS CUP

After the 1977-78 season had ended, Wrexham played Blyth Spartans in the two-legged Debenhams Cup Final, a competition for the FA Cup's biggest giant killers. The Robins had reached the sixth round where they lost 3-2 to Arsenal. Their opponents took Wrexham to two games in the fifth round before a Graham Whittle penalty gave the Robins victory in the replay at St James' Park, Newcastle.

In the first leg of the Debenhams Cup, Whittle scored again but the Spartans won 2-1 at the Racecourse Ground. In the second leg in the north-east the game ended all-square at 1-1 with Lyons netting for Wrexham to give Blyth Spartans a 3-2 aggregate victory.

DEBUTS

The club's youngest debutante is Ken Roberts who was 15 years 158 days old when he played at Bradford Park Avenue on 1st September 1951.

Though there have been a number of Wrexham players who have scored on their debut, none have scored a quicker debut goal than Bernard Evans who netted after 25 seconds of the Robins' 2-2 draw at Bradford City on 15th September 1954.

DEFEATS – FEWEST

During the 1977-78 and 1992-93 seasons, Wrexham went through the respective 46 and 42 match programmes suffering only eight defeats as they won the Third Division championship in 1977-78 and were runners-up to Cardiff City in the Third Division in 1992-93.

DEFEATS – MOST

Wrexham's total of 27 defeats during the 1963-64 season is the worst in the club's history. Not surprisingly they finished 23rd in the Third Division and were relegated.

DEFEATS – WORST

Wrexham's record defeat was when Brentford beat them 9-0 at Griffin Park on 15th October 1963. At the end of that season the Robins finished 23rd in the Third Division and were relegated. The club also had nine goal put past them in the third round of the FA Cup in 1930-31 when they lost 9-1 against Wolverhampton Wanderers at Molineux.

During the 1941-42 Football Regional League North Division, Wrexham were beaten 10-3 by Manchester United in a game played at Maine Road.

DEFENSIVE RECORDS

Wrexham's best defensive record was established in 1978-79. They conceded just 42 goals in that campaign and finished 15th in the Second Division. The Robins' worst defensive record was in 1963-64 when they let in 107 goals to finish 23rd in the Third Division and were relegated to Division Four.

DISMISSALS

Brian Simpson was the first Wrexham player to be sent-off in a League game when he received his marching orders in a 2-1 win at Southport on 28th January 1922, during the club's inaugural season in the competition.

One of the quickest sending-off occurred on Christmas Day 1936 when Wrexham inside-forward Ambrose Brown was dismissed after just 20 seconds of the Robins' 2-1 home defeat by Chester.

One of the strangest dismissals befell Dixie McNeil when on 19th January 1980, he was sent off as he was waiting to take a penalty-kick for Wrexham against Charlton Athletic. With the scores level at 2-2 on the Racecourse Ground, Wrexham were awarded a penalty in the closing minutes and visiting players first protested and then indulged in some gamesmanship tactics while McNeil was waiting to take the kick. Eventually, McNeil's patience snapped and he kicked the ball into the crowd and was promptly sent off by the referee who had booked him earlier in the match. It was left to Mick Vinter to score from the spot and give Wrexham a 3-2 win.

DRAWS

Wrexham played their greatest number of drawn League matches in a single season in 1966-67 and 1986-87 when 20 of their matches ended all -square and their fewest in 1933-34 when only five of their matches were drawn.

The club's highest scoring draw in the Football League is 4-4, a score line in five games – Rochdale (Away 1928-29), Gateshead (Away 1932-33), Oldham Athletic (Home 1956-57), Peterborough United (Home 1962-63) and Plymouth Argyle (Home 1996-97).

Other 4-4 draws have been in the FA Cup against Bristol City (Away 1977-78); the Welsh Cup against Swansea Town (Away 1954-55); The Football Regional League against Stoke City (Home 1939-40) and Tranmere Rovers (Away 1942-43) and in the Combination League against Rhyl (Away 1902-03).

However, the club did play in a 5-5 draw at home to West Bromwich Albion in the Football Regional League North Division match on 3rd January 1942.

DWYER, ALAN

Liverpool-born Alan Dwyer was playing for Halewood Youth Club when he was invited to the Racecourse Ground for trials. After signing as an apprentice he worked his way up through the ranks and made his first team debut in a Welsh Cup win over Blaenau Flestiniog in January 1974, scoring in a 6-3 win. However, he had another nine months to wait before playing in his first Football League game when he came on as a substitute for Brian Tinnion in a 3-3 draw at Brighton and Hove Albion.

In his early days with the Robins, Dwyer played in midfield, but was later switched to left-back, where he gave a number of polished performances. Though a series of niggling injuries were to restrict his number of appearances for the club, he only missed one game in the 1977-78 season when the club won the Third Division championship. Also that season he won a Welsh Cup winners' medal as Wrexham beat Bangor City 3-1 on aggregate.

He went on to make 239 first team appearances for the club before leaving to join Bury in the summer of 1981. He later ended his League career with Stockport County before playing non-League football for Oswestry Town, Runcorn and Chirk AAA where he was also later manager.

Alan Dwyer

E

EDWARDS, IAN

Ian Edwards turned down an apprenticeship with Wrexham and joined West Bromwich Albion. Though he scored on his League debut, he found his chances limited and in November 1976, he joined Chester for a fee of £20,000.

Whilst with the then Sealand Road club he won the first of his four Welsh caps against Kuwait and on his next appearance at full international level he scored four goals in a 7-0 win over Malta. For Chester he scored 36 goals in 104 League games before in November 1979, he joined Wrexham for a fee of £125,000.

He made his League debut in a 1-0 defeat at West Ham United and though he suffered from injuries towards the end of that 1979-80 campaign, he did score a hat-trick in a 5-0 Welsh Cup win over Connah's Quay Nomads. When the Robins lost their Second Division status in 1981-82, Edwards was the leading League goal-scorer with 11 goals. In July 1982, after having scored 30 goals in 99 appearances in three years at the Racecourse Ground he joined Crystal Palace.

Sadly, the knee problem he had throughout most of his career curtailed his playing days after just 18 League appearances and four goals for the Selhurst Park club.

Ian Edwards

EUROPEAN CUP WINNERS' CUP

Wrexham have participated in the European Cup Winners' Cup on eight occasions.

The first was in 1972-73 when they were paired with FC Zurich of Switzerland. In the away leg, the Robins came away with a creditable 1-1 draw with Albert Kinsey scoring the club's first goal in Europe. In the return leg, goals from Billy Ashcroft and Mel Sutton gave Wrexham a 2-1 win on the night and 3-2 on aggregate. In the second round, Yugoslavian Hajduk Split were Wrexham's opponents and after the Welsh club won the first leg at the Racecourse Ground 3-1 with Brian Tinnion scoring two of the goals, hopes that the club would progress into the quarter-finals were quite high. Sadly, Wrexham lost 2-0 and went out on the away-goals rule.

In 1975-76, the Robins became the first Third Division team to reach the quarter-finals of the European Cup Winners' Cup. In the first round they beat Swedish side Djurgardens IF 2-1 at the Racecourse Ground and then drew 1-1 in Sweden to go through. In round two, Stal Rzeszow of Poland were beaten 2-0 with both goals scored by Billy Ashcroft before a Mel Sutton goal gave the Robins a 1-1 draw. The quarter-finals saw Wrexham paired with RSC Anderlecht of Belgium. The Belgian side was full of internationals but only managed a 1-0 win on home soil. A crowd of almost 20,000 packed into the Racecourse for the return and though the Belgian 'keeper was in fine form, he was finally beaten by Stuart Lee. Unfortunately for Wrexham, Resenbrink equalised to take Anderlecht through 2-1 on aggregate. The Belgian side went on to win the trophy.

In the Cup Winners' Cup competition of 1978-79, the Robins went out at the first hurdle 3-2 to Yugoslavian side NK Rijeka, this after they had lost the first leg 3-0. The following season also saw the Robins knocked out in the first round when German side IFC Magdeburg won 7-5 on aggregate after extra-time.

In 1984-85, a Jim Steel goal gave Wrexham a 1-0 home win over FC Porto but in Portugal, the home side were far too good for the Welsh club and raced into a 3-0 lead. The Robins then proceeded to produce one of the greatest comebacks in the history of the club when two goals from Jake King made it 3-2. Porto then scored a fourth before Barry Horne netted in the last minute to send the Welsh club through to the second round on the away-goals rule. Facing AS Roma, Wrex-

Celebrating at the RSC Anderlecht vs Wrexham quarter final

ham lost 2-0 in Italy and 1-0 at the Racecourse Ground, though on both occasions the Robins put up a brave display.

In 1986-87, Maltese side FC Zurrieq were beaten 7-0 on aggregate with Steve Massey scoring three goals over the two legs. In the second round, a fine rearguard action helped the Robins to a goal-less draw at Real Zaragoza whilst in the home leg, the tie ended all-square at 2-2 but the Spaniards went through on the away goals rule.

The Cup Winners' Cup competition of 1990-91 saw Wrexham held to a goal-less draw at home by Danish club Lyngby BK before a Chris Armstrong goal in Denmark was enough to take the Robins through to the next round where they were drawn to play Manchester United. The first leg at Old Trafford saw United win 3-0 and though the Welsh club lost 2-0 at home, they were not disgraced. The Red Devils went on to win the trophy beating Barcelona in the final.

The last time Wrexham were involved in the European Cup Winners' Cup was 1995-96 when they went out in the first round to Petrolul Plolesti of Romania 1-0 on aggregate.

EVANS, GEORGE

Signed from Cheshire League side Oswestry Town in the summer of 1955, George Evans spent the next two seasons still playing in the Cheshire League for Wrexham Reserves.

He made his first team debut on 19th October 1957, in a 3-1 home win over Hartlepool United but had to wait until towards the end of that season before establishing a regular place in the Wrexham side. His only goal that season was the club's second in a 2-1 win at York City but he did play in the side that beat Chester after a replay to win the Welsh Cup. Over the next few seasons, Evans made a number of significant contributions to Wrexham's successes, helping them to the fourth round of the League Cup in 1960-61 and promotion to the Third Division the following season.

Towards the end of the 1962-63 season he was facing stiff competition at wing-half from Tecwyn Jones and in the close season joined Chester in exchange for Billy Myrescough. Evans, who had played in 208 League and Cup games for Wrexham, stayed five years at Sealand Road before playing non-League football for Bethesda and Colwyn Bay.

EVANS, MICKEY

A former Welsh Schoolboy and Youth international, he began his career with Wolverhampton Wanderers but after two years with the Molineux club in which he never progressed further than their Central League side, he was given a free transfer.

Wrexham manager Jack Rowley brought Evans to the Racecourse Ground in the summer of 1966 and he made his debut in a goal-less draw at home to Exeter City on the opening day of the 1966-67 season. In his first season with the club, Evans played at inside-forward and in 43 League and Cup games scored 13 goals including a hat-trick in a 5-0 Welsh Cup victory over Rhyl. After that he showed his great versatility in playing virtually every other position for the club including a second-half spell in goal in the match against Aston Villa on 26th September 1970, following an injury to Dave Gaskell. For the record, Villa won 3-2.

In his time with Wrexham, Evans helped the club win promotion to the Third Division in 1969-70 and to the Second Division as champions in 1977-78. He also won three Welsh Cup winners' medals and was selected for the Welsh Under-23 side on four occasions.

In only his second game in Division Two, Evans was stretchered off in the 1-0 victory at Fulham and though he tried to make a comeback, he made just three more appearances before being forced to quit the game. Evans who had played in 476 first team games, then worked as a coach at the Racecourse Ground before becoming assistant-manager to Mel Sutton. Following the club's relegation to the Third Division in 1981ß82, his contract was not renewed and he joined Caersws as manager.

EVER-PRESENTS

There have been 38 Wrexham players who have been ever-present throughout a Football League season. The greatest number of ever-present seasons by a Wrexham player is seven by Alf Jones. Next in line is Brian Lloyd with five.

F

FA CUP

Wrexham entered the FA Cup for the first time in 1883-84 and were drawn at home against Liverpool Ramblers in the first round. However, on the morning of the match, the club received a telegram stating that the Ramblers could not raise a team and therefore would have to scratch. In the second round Wrexham entertained Oswestry and went down 4-3 at the Racecourse Ground. The Shropshire club's winning goal was disputed by the entire Wrexham team and the referee had to have a police escort at the end of the match.

In 1973-74, Wrexham beat Shrewsbury Town 1-0 at Gay Meadow in the first round after the original tie had ended all-square at 1-1 at the Racecourse Ground. In round two, Rotherham United were easily beaten 3-0 and then Second Division Crystal Palace were swept aside 2-0 at Selhurst Park. In the fourth round, Wrexham travelled to Ayresome Park to face Middlesbrough who were then the leaders of the Second Division but won 1-0 thanks to a David Smallman goal. Smallman was again the hero in round five as the Robins beat First Division Southampton 1-0 at The Dell. In the sixth round for the first time in their history, Wrexham were drawn away to Burnley and though they gave of their best, they lost 1-0 with the Clarets goals taking a wicked deflection off the heel of David Fogg.

In 1977-78 after beating Burton United and Preston North End both by a 2-0 score line, Wrexham took two First Division scalps in Bristol City, who were beaten 3-0 after a pulsating 4-4 draw and Newcastle United 4-1 also after a replay. Drawn against non-League Blyth Spartans in round five, it was the Welsh club's turn to come back from the dead, snatching an equaliser in the 88th minute and winning the replay. The second match attracted so much attention that Blyth switched the game to St James' Park to accommodate a 42,000 crowd. The Robins then went down 3-2 to Arsenal in the sixth round with Dixie McNeil, who netted Wrexham's first goal, having scored in every round of that season's competition.In 1991-92, Wrexham beat Winsford United 5-2 with Steve Watkin netting a hat-trick and then defeated another non-League side Telford United 1-0 with Watkin again the hero. In round three, Wrexham, who had finished bottom of the Fourth Division the previous season beat League Champions Arsenal 2-1 at the Racecourse Ground with Watkin and Thomas the scorers. Drawn against more top flight opposition in West Ham United, the Robins drew 2-2 at Upton Park before going down 1-0 at home in the replay.

The club last reached the sixth round in 1996-97. After drawing 1-1 at Colwyn Bay, the Robins won the replay 2-0 with Bryan Hughes scoring all Wrexham's goals in the tie. The Welsh club also took two games to get through the second round, winning 3-2 at Scunthorpe United after extra-time, following a 2-2 draw at the Racecourse Ground. The third round saw Wrexham entertain Premiership side West Ham United and Hughes kept up his record of scoring in every round in a 1-1 draw. In the replay at Upton Park, a 90th minute winner from substitute Kevin Russell gave Wrexham a place in the fifth round at Peterborough United. In a high scoring game, Russell who had kept his place, scored two goals in a 4-2 win. Despite going a goal behind to Birmingham City in the fifth round, goals from Hughes, Humes and Connolly took the Robins through to the sixth round for the third time in their history, but sadly they lost 1-0 at Chesterfield, who themselves were unlucky not to reach Wembley after taking Middlesbrough to a replay.

FATHER AND SON

Cliff Lloyd who played a great part in the history of Wrexham Football Club as a player, secretary and manager had three sons, two of which, Geoff and John Lloyd both played League football for the Robins, though never in the same Wrexham line-up.

FIRST LEAGUE MATCH

Wrexham played their first-ever Football League match at the Racecourse Ground on 27th August 1921. Their opponents were Hartlepool United and a crowd of 8,000 turned up to witness the occasion.The Robins almost scored straight from the kick-off but as Noel Edwards shaped up to shoot, Hartlepool's Crilly robbed him of the ball. Ernie Lloyd then went close for the home side but after 20 minutes and against the run of play, Mulholland opened the scoring for Hartlepool, chipping the ball over the advancing Godding after Robert Griffiths had made a bad clearance.

Noel Edwards went close again for Wrexham but five minutes before half-time, the visitors scored again when Lister, who was completely unmarked shot past Godding.

In the second half, Wrexham created a number of chances, the best of which fell to Bill Cotton, but they still couldn't break down a stubborn Hartlepool defence.

The Wrexham team for that historic match was: G. Godding; J. Ellis; R. Simpson; T. Mathias; B. Foster; R. Griffiths; M. Burton; B. Goode; B. Cotton; N. Edwards and E. Lloyd.

FIRST MATCHES

The first match to be arranged was played at the Cricket Ground on Saturday 5th October 1872, when two teams comprising of members of the newly formed Wrexham Football Club played a game between themselves. The result of that match was a 2-2 draw.

Two weeks later, the club played its first match against other opposition when they beat Grove Park School past and present members in a 12-a-side game, 2-0.

FLOODLIGHTS

In 1959, floodlights were added to the Racecourse Ground at a cost of £14,000, the money being raised by the Supporters' Club. The club's first floodlit game at the Racecourse Ground took place on 30th September 1959, when a crowd of 15,555 turned up to witness the event. Sadly, Wrexham lost 2-1 to Swindon Town with Stan Bennion scoring for the home side.

FLYNN, BRIAN

A Welsh Schoolboy international, he was first spotted playing for Neath Boys by Cardiff City, but the Ninian Park club let him slip through the net, enabling Burnley to sign him as an apprentice in 1971 and then as a professional on his 17th birthday the following year.

After making his League debut for the Clarets at Arsenal in 1974 he began to establish himself in the Turf Moor club's midfield.

At only 19 years of age, Brian Flynn won the first of 66 Welsh caps in a win over Luxembourg in the European Championships at Vetch Field in November 1974.

After Burnley were relegated to the Second Division in 1976, Flynn joined Leeds United for £175,000 and immediately forged a superb midfield partnership with England international Tony Currie. After scoring 11 goals in 154 games for the Elland Road club he rejoined Burnley in November 1982, after a brief loan spell at the club.

He left for Cardiff City in 1984 and after spells with Doncaster Rovers and Bury, he became player-coach at Limerick. Another spell at Belle Vue followed and then after working with the PFA's Football in the Community Scheme at Burnley, he moved to the Racecourse Ground in February 1988.

He made his League debut in a 3-2 home defeat by Torquay United at the end of that month and went on to play in 132 first team games

Brian Flynee

for the club before hanging up his boots, including the four play-off games at the end of the 1988-89 season. When McNeil resigned as Wrexham manager, Flynn was asked to take over as player-manager. After two fairly traumatic campaigns and finishing bottom of the League in 1990-91, Flynn began to turn things around and in 1992-93 led the club to promotion to the new Second Division.

Since then, the club have come close to the play-offs on a number of occasions, perhaps none more so than in 1997-98 when they finished seventh, as Flynn, a player who has performed at the very highest level, demonstrated that he has the credentials to go to the top in football management.

FOGG, DAVE

Liverpool-born full-back Dave Fogg worked his way through the junior ranks at Wrexham before making his first team debut in a 2-2 draw at Plymouth Argyle in February 1971. Despite giving a competent display, his next appearance at this level wasn't for another twelve months when the Devon club were once again Wrexham's opponents.

Dave Fogg

After that he became a first team regular and was ever-present in 1973-74 when the Robins finished fourth in Division Three. Also that season he played in all the games in the club's run to the sixth round of the FA Cup where they lost 1-0 at Burnley. During his time at the Racecourse Ground, he won two Welsh Cup winners' medals in 1972 and 1975 and played in 202 first team matches. His only goal in Wrexham colours came in the 6-3 Welsh Cup win over Blaenau Ffestiniog in January 1974.

After leaving the Robins he joined Oxford United and helped the Manor Ground club to win promotion from the Third to the First Division in successive seasons. He appeared in 293 league games for the U's but missed their Milk Cup victory in 1986. He later became assistant-manager to Brian Horton at Oxford before becoming youth coach at Everton.

FOOTBALL LEAGUE CUP

Sad to relate, Wrexham have failed to make much impact upon the Football League (later Milk, Littlewoods, Rumbelows and Coca Cola) Cup with the exception of 1977-78 when as a Third Division side they reached the fifth round.

Wrexham's first match in the League Cup on 18th October 1960, saw them draw 1-1 at Northampton Town before winning the replay 2-0. Brighton were then beaten by the same score line before a Mickey Metcalf goal gave the Robins a 1-1 draw at First Division Blackburn Rovers. In the replay at the Racecourse Ground, Mickey Metcalf hit a superb hat-trick as the Fourth Division side produced a historic 3-1 victory. Sadly, in the fourth round, the Robins travelled to play Aston Villa and were soundly beaten 5-0.

After that the club failed to make much headway and in 1966-67 were beaten 6-1 by Shrewsbury Town. In 1971-72 they took Aston Villa to three matches before losing 4-3 in the second replay at The Hawthorns. The following season, Wrexham produced their biggest victory in the competition when they beat Crewe Alexandra 4-0. The club had won through to the fourth round again in 1976-77 before their bogey team Aston Villa again knocked them out of the competition, winning 5-1 at Villa Park.

In 1977-78 the Robins reached the fifth round for the only time in their history. They beat Stockport County 2-1 on aggregate in the first round before an own goal helped them to a late victory at Charlton Athletic in the next round. A Bobby Shinton goal was enough to give them a 1-0 third round victory over Bristol City and then goals from Lyons and Whittle helped the Robins beat Swindon Town 2-0. In the fifth round, a crowd of 25,641 turned up at the Racecourse Ground for the match against Liverpool which the Anfield side won 3-1.

Since then, the furthest the club have been is the third round in 1981-82 and in 1990-91, the Robins lost 11-0 on aggregate to Everton!

FOUNDATION

Wrexham are the oldest club in Wales still in existence. Though the club have accepted 1873 as the year they were founded, Peter Jones in his splendid book 'Wrexham A Complete Record 1872-1992' has revealed that the club were in fact founded on 28th September 1872. By 1875, Wrexham's team formation, which had varied between 12 and 17-a-side was reduced to 11 men and a year later they were among the founders of the Welsh FA.

FOURTH DIVISION

Wrexham have had three spells in the Fourth Division. After relegation from the Third Division in 1959-60, Billy Morris took over as team boss but after the club's first game in the League basement saw them lose 3-0 at Peterborough United, they failed to improve and had to settle for 16th place.

For the 1961-62 season, Ken Barnes was appointed the club's new player-manager and in his first season took the Robins back to the Third Division. The highlight of the season was undoubtedly the club's record score of 10-1 against Hartlepool United, a match in which Wyn Davies, Roy Ambler and Ron Barnes all netted hat-tricks.

The club's second spell in the Fourth Division lasted six seasons from 1964-65 to 1969-70. In 1965-66 the Robins finished the season in 92nd place in the Football League for the first time in their history. During the club's promotion winning season of 1969-70, they only lost three of their first 21 matches to finish as runners-up to Chesterfield.

The club's last and longest spell in the Fourth Division began in 1983-84 after successive relegation's from the Second and Third Divisions. In 1990-91 the Robins again finished in last place in the Football League but were spared the ignominy of automatic relegation as membership was increased from 92 to 94 clubs. Following the reorganisation of the Football League in 1992-93, Wrexham finished runners-up in the new Third Division to move out of the League's basement.

FOX, ALAN

Alan Fox joined Wrexham from Carmel United in the summer of 1953 and made his first team debut whilst still an amateur in a 2-1 win at Crewe Alexandra in April 1954, when replacing the injured Ron Wynn. He began his career as a right-half but soon moved to centre-half where between 1956 and 1964 he was one of the best centre-halves in the lower divisions.

He was an ever-present in seasons 1958-59, 1960-61 and 1961-62 and at one stage appeared in 163 consecutive league games.

In 1959 he was capped at Under-23 level against Scotland at the Racecourse Ground and in 1961-62 helped the club win promotion. During that campaign he scored the first of his three goals for the club to help the Robins beat Bradford City 2-1. Fox also won three Welsh Cup winners' medals in 1957, 1958 and 1960. Following the club's relegation in 1963-64, Fox was surprisingly allowed to join Hartlepool United on a free transfer after having played in 414 games for the Racecourse Ground club.

After 58 League appearances for Hartlepool, he ended his League career with Bradford City before becoming player-coach of Irish club, Dundalk.

FOX, STEVE

The son of a former Gillingham player, he began his career with his home-town team Tamworth in the Southern League before joining Birmingham City. Though he soon broke into the senior side at St Andrew's, he could not gain a place on a regular basis and after appearing in 29 league games joined Wrexham for a fee of £95,000 in December 1978.

Steve Fox

He made his debut in a 2-1 defeat at Preston North End on Boxing Day and soon became a great favourite with the Wrexham supporters. His exciting wing play made him an automatic choice over the next three and a half seasons and he went on to score 19 goals in 181 first team matches.There was no doubting Steve Fox's ability but after the club were relegated to the Third Division in 1981-82, he played in a handful of matches before being allowed to join Port Vale. In his first season with the Valiants, he helped them win promotion from the Fourth Division but after 82 League and Cup appearances he joined Chester City. After his contract was cancelled in October 1985, he helped out Llangollen.

FREIGHT ROVER TROPHY

A competition designed solely and specifically for Associate Members of the Football League, the Freight Rover Trophy replaced the initial Associate Members Cup for the 1984-85 season.

Having already been knocked out of the FA Cup and League Cup competitions by Wigan Athletic, the Robins got their chance for revenge when paired with the Springfield Park club in the first round of the 1984-85 Freight Rover Trophy. A crowd of just 765 saw the sides draw 2-2 at the Racecourse Ground before the Latics won the second leg 3-1 to complete a hat-trick of defeats over Wrexham in that season's cup competitions.

In 1985-86, the Robins drew both of their group games, 1-1 at home to Port Vale and 2-2 at Blackpool with both goals scored by Steve Charles, but failed to progress to the knockout stages.

The following season saw Wrexham almost make it to the Wembley final. In their group games, the Robins beat Tranmere Rovers 6-1 and then drew 2-2 at Wigan Athletic to qualify for the knockout stages. The scorers in that draw at Springfield Park were Buxton and Charles and they were on the score sheet again in the club's 2-1 first round win at Scunthorpe United. In the Northern Area quarter-final they defeated Preston North End 2-1 to reach the semi-final where they played Chester City. In a game watched by 5,662, by far the biggest gate of the club's run to this stage of the competition, Wrexham were leading 1-0 courtesy of a Paul Comstive goal when the referee awarded a rather dubious penalty to Chester with just minutes remaining. The spot-kick was converted and the game went into extra-time where two further goals for Chester saw them go through 3-1.

G

GASKELL, DAVE

An England Schoolboy and Youth international, Dave Gaskell became a Manchester United junior in 1955, turning professional two years later on his 17th birthday after having already played for the senior side against Manchester City in the 1956 FA Charity Shield game.

Though he squeezed most of his 137 League appearances for United in between the lengthy careers of Harry Gregg and Alex Stepney, he did keep goal in the 1963 FA Cup Final against Leicester City and played in Europe, as well as winning England Under-23 honours.

Dave Gaskell

He joined Wrexham in the summer of 1969 after a lengthy loan spell with then non-League Wigan Athletic and made his debut in a 3-0 home win against Exeter City on the opening day of the 1969-70 season. In his first season at the Racecourse Ground, he kept 16 clean sheets in 45 games and helped the Robins finish runners-up to Chesterfield and so win promotion to the Third Division.

On 11th January

1971, the Wigan-born 'keeper scored from the penalty spot in a 6-3 Welsh Cup win over Porthmadoc but by the end of the following season, Gaskell had left Wrexham after making 117 appearances.

GIANTKILLERS

As mentioned in the FA Cup entry, Wrexham performed one of the greatest of giant-killing acts on 4 January 1992 when they beat the previous season's League Champions Arsenal at the Racecourse Ground 2-1. The Gunners took the lead two minutes before the interval through Alan Smith and nearly increased their lead in the 62nd minute when Nigel Winterburn's shot hit the underside of the bar. Then in two unbelievable minutes, Arsenal's world fell apart. In the 82nd minute, Wrexham were awarded a free kick some 20 yards out. Mickey Thomas took the free kick, the ball flying straight into David Seaman's top right-hand corner. The Robins' fans' cheers could still be heard when Tony Adams fumbled a clearance from Gordon Davies' cross and Steve Watkin poked the ball past Seaman. The Wrexham team on that glorious day was: O'Keefe; Thackeray; Hardy; Carey; Thomas; Sertori; Davies; Owen; Connolly; Watkin; Phillips;

GOALKEEPERS

Wrexham Football Club has almost always been extremely well served by its goalkeepers and most of them have been highly popular with the supporters.

Tracey Morgan who joined the club from Druids, arrived at the Racecourse Ground with a reputation for saving penalties. He was a member of the Wrexham side that in 1904-05 won both the Combination League and Welsh Cup.

The club's first 'keeper in the Football League was George Godding. He made his league debut in Wrexham's inaugural match against Hartlepool United and went on to become the first Wrexham player to complete 100 League appearances. Capped twice by Wales he played in 188 games for the club.

In a year from 1952, Wrexham had goalkeepers born in four different countries – Bob Connor (English) Archie Ferguson (Scottish) Bill Hayes (Irish) and Earl Godding, the son of George (Welsh).

Kevin Keelan who made his name with Norwich City helped the

club win promotion from the Fourth to the Third Division in 1961-62, his first season with the club and Dave Gaskell, who began his career with Manchester United actually scored for the Robins. His goal for the Robins came in the 6-3 Welsh Cup victory over Porthmadoc when he netted from the penalty spot.

Brian Lloyd made a record 248 consecutive League appearances in the Wrexham goal and 312 consecutive appearances including all games. Dai Davies who was capped 52 times by Wales joined Wrexham from Everton for a fee of £8,000 in September 1977, proved to be a real bargain. He was a virtual ever-present in the club's Second Division side and in two seasons of European competition.

The club's present goalkeeper is Andy Marriott. Signed from Nottingham Forest, he played in 143 consecutive games from his debut and won his first full cap for Wales against Switzerland in April 1996.

GOALS

The most goals Wrexham have ever scored in one game is 11, a feat they have achieved on three occasions. The first came on 27th October 1894, when Caergwle were beaten 11-1 in a Welsh League game. On 9th September 1911, Wrexham beat Rhyl 11-0 in an FA Cup preliminary round match and on 3rd January 1934, the Robins beat New Brighton 11-1 in a Football League North Section Cup game.

In the Football League, Wrexham beat Hartlepool United 10-1 on 3rd March 1962, on their way to winning promotion from the Fourth Division.

GOALS – CAREER BEST

The highest goal-scorer in the club's history is Tommy Bamford who between season 1928-29 and the end of 1934-35 netted 201 goals for the club. These comprised of 174 League goals, 10 in the FA Cup and 17 in the Welsh Cup.

GOALS – INDIVIDUAL

Two Wrexham players have scored five goals in a game, Bert Goode and Tommy Bamford, who, performed the feat on two occasions.

Bert Goode scored five goals on 7th January 1911, as Wrexham beat Chirk 9-0 in the first round of the Welsh Cup. Tommy Bamford first scored five goals on 3rd January 1934, as the Robins beat New Brighton 11-1 in a Football League Northern Section Cup first round match. Later that season he repeated the feat in the Football League as Carlisle United were beaten 8-1 on 17th March 1934.

GOALS – SEASON

The club's highest League goal-scorer in any one season is Tommy Bamford who scored 44 League goals as Wrexham finished sixth in the Third Division (North) in 1933-34. He scored five goals against Carlisle United (Home 8-1), four against Doncaster Rovers (Away 4-1) and hat-tricks against Mansfield Town (Home 5-0) Gateshead (Away 3-0) and Walsall (Home 4-2).

GODDING, GEORGE

Goalkeeper George Godding joined Wrexham from Cheshire League side Crichton Athletic in April 1921, as the Robins attempted to build a squad capable of holding its own in the Football League.

He made his League debut at home to Hartlepool United on 27th August 1921, in the club's first game in the competition after having played in two FA Cup matches against Witton Albion in 1919 when Fred Boxley was unavailable.

In 1923, the Caergwrle-born 'keeper won two full caps for Wales when he played against Scotland and Ireland. On 9th February 1924, when Wrexham drew 0-0 at New Brighton, Godding became the first Wrexham player to complete 100 League appearances for the club.

He also won two Welsh Cup winners' medals in 1924 and 1925 but at the end of the 1925-26 season after he had played in 188 first team games he left the Racecourse Ground to join Llandudno Town in the Welsh League. Godding later ended his career with Oak Alyn Rovers.

GOODE, BERT

One of the greatest forwards ever to play for Wrexham, Chester-born Bert Goode played his early football with a number of local clubs, namely Old St Mary', Hoole and Saltney before joining Chester in 1907. After a number of impressive performances he signed for Liverpool but failed to settle at Anfield and in the summer of 1910 he joined Wrexham.

He made his debut in the opening game of the 1910-11 season in the Birmingham and District League, scoring one of the goals in a 4-1 win at Halesowen. He went on to be the club's leading scorer with 25 goals in 33 League games including hat-tricks against Worcester City (Home 4-1), West Bromwich Albion Reserves (Home 6-2) and Stoke (Home 7-1). In that season's Welsh Cup competition he scored five goals in a 9-0 first round win over Chirk and a hat-trick in the final as Wrexham beat Connah's Quay 6-0.

At the end of his first season in which he scored 37 goals in 39 games he was transferred to Aston Villa but after just seven games he left to join Hull City. Feeling homesick, he returned to the Racecourse Ground for the start of the 1913-14 season and again top-scored with 26 goals in all competitions including hat-tricks against Dudley (Home 5-0) in the Birmingham and District League and Newtown (Home 7-0) in the Welsh Cup. In 1914-15 he netted another hat-trick in the 3-1 Welsh Cup win at Llandudno and went on to win his third Welsh Cup winners' medal. He was the club's leading scorer in 1919-20 and the following season, netted two more hat-tricks against Wednesbury Old Athletic (Home 6-0) in the Birmingham and District League and Northwich Victoria (Home 3-0) in the FA Cup.

He played in the club's inaugural match in the Football League and went on to appear in 276 first team games, scoring 137 goals. His last League game in October 1925, saw him score one of Wrexham's goals in a 6-5 home defeat by Accrington Stanley!

GREGORY, DAVID

David Gregory was released from his home-town club Peterborough United for being too small but after impressing in non-League football, he was given another chance by Posh boss, Noel Cantwell. After four years at London Road in which he scored 32 goals in 142 League games, he was transferred to Stoke City for a fee of £55,000. Within twelve months he had left the Victoria Ground after a series of disagreements over what was his best position and after a loan spell with Blackburn Rovers in which he scored three goals in five games, he joined Bury. After two years at Gigg Lane he moved to Portsmouth, netting 18 goals in 74 League games for the Fratton Park club.

Gregory was given a free transfer by the south coast club and in August 1982, joined Wrexham. He played his first game for the Rob-

1982 signing of David Gregory

ins in a 2-1 win at Cardiff City on the opening day of the 1982-83 season and though he turned in some fine performances, he couldn't prevent the club being relegated for the second successive season. In 1983-84 he was the club's leading scorer with 23 goals including a hat-trick on the last day of the season as Tranmere Rovers were beaten 5-1. He went on to score 45 goals in 194 first team outings before returning to his first club, Peterborough United. He had scored 40 goals in 173 League games in his two spells with Posh before entering non-League football with King's Lynn.

GRIFFITHS, ARFON

Arfon Griffiths joined Wrexham straight from school, turning professional in May 1959. He made his League debut for the Racecourse club in a 2-1 home win over Reading in November 1959, and went on to score eight goals in 42 League appearances before he was transferred to Arsenal for £15,000 in February 1961.

He made his debut for the Gunners in a 5-1 defeat at Wolverhampton Wanderers at the end of the 1960-61 season before playing in 14 games, mainly as a scheming inside-forward the following campaign. Unable to maintain his first team place, he was subsequently transferred back to his old club Wrexham for £8,000.

Arfon Griffiths was a loyal servant to Wrexham and over the next 17 seasons, appeared in 713 first team games. At Arsenal he had made two appearances for the Welsh Under-23 team and on his return to the Racecourse Ground gained two more Under-23 caps and made 17 full appearances for Wales. The first of these came

Arfon Griffiths

in 1971 when he came on as a substitute against Czechoslovakia, the remainder between 1975 and 1977.

He scored 120 League goals for the Robins, second only to Tommy Bamford in the club's all-time scoring charts.

His best season for the club was undoubtedly 1969-70 when he masterminded the club's promotion to the Third Division and scored 16 goals in 44 games.

In 1975, John Neal appointed him as his assistant-manager and when he left to manage Middlesbrough, the Wrexham board had no hesitation in appointing Griffiths as his successor. In his first season in charge, he led the club to the Third Division championship and Welsh Cup and over the next four years kept the club in the Second Division. In the summer of 1981, he resigned his post following an internal disagreement but soon returned to management with Crewe Alexandra.

The Gresty Road club finished bottom of the Football League in 1981-82 and were still bottom when he was sacked in October 1982.

Awarded the MBE for his services to football, he returned to Wrexham to open a newsagent's shop and has not involved himself with football since.

GUEST PLAYERS

The 'guest' system was used by all clubs during the two wars. Although at times it was abused almost beyond belief (in that some sides that opposed Wrexham had ten or 11 'guest'!) it normally worked sensibly and effectively to the benefit of players, clubs and supporters alike.

The most distinguished players to 'guest' for the Robins were Stanley Matthews, Stan Cullis, Ronnie Dix, Jackie Milburn, and John Hancocks, all England internationals and Tommy G. Jones of Wales.

GUNSON, GORDON

He began his career with Cheshire junior side Brickfield's before entering League football with Nelson, who were then in the Third Division (North). In the summer of 1926, he joined Wrexham and made his debut in a 3-1 home win over Chesterfield on the opening day of the 1926-27 season. The following campaign he scored 17 League and Cup goals including a hat-trick in a 5-0 win over Barrow at the Racecourse Ground. In 1928-29 he was an ever-present and scored 18 League and Cup goals including a spell of five in four games as Wrexham finished third in Division Three (North). His outstanding form won him selection for the Welsh team before he pointed out that he was born in Chester!

Gunson had scored 40 goals in 116 first team games, when in June 1929, he left the Racecourse Ground to sign for Sunderland, who paid £1,500 for his services.

His stay at Roker Park was a short one because in November 1930, he signed for Liverpool. Gunson was a first team regular at Anfield and made 87 League appearances scoring 26 goals before being injured. He then had a short spell with Swindon Town before returning to play for Wrexham. Sadly, he was only able to play in a further 15 games before the injury he sustained with Liverpool forced his retirement from League football.

He became player-manager of Bangor City and managed Flint Town and after the war, was appointed trainer at Crewe Alexandra.

H

HARDY, PHIL

Phil Hardy

The Ellesmere Port-born full-back made his debut for Wrexham in the final game of the 1989-90 season when the Robins were beaten 2-1 at home by Hartlepool United.

Captain of the Republic of Ireland Under-21 team, he made the left-back berth his own and was ever-present in 1991-92 when he was voted into the PFA Fourth Division team. Over the past eight seasons he has continued to give solid performances in the Wrexham defence. Known at the Racecourse Ground as the 'Hardy Perennial', he has appeared in 346 first team games, though he has yet to score a goal at this level!

Though he seems to have been at Wrexham for a long time, Hardy is only 25 and though he has been hampered by injuries and the form of the ever-improving Deryn Brace, he remains an important member of the Welsh club's squad.

HARRISON, BILLY

Though he was born in Ireland, Billy Harrison moved to Wales when he was a young boy and began his football career playing as a centre-forward for Wrexham Gymnasium. In 1893 he joined Wrexham but he had to wait until the 1894-95 season before making his first team debut in a 6-1 defeat at Chirk on the opening day of the season. Despite that setback, Wrexham went on to win the Welsh League and Harrison scored 14 goals including four in a 7-2 home win over Rhostyllen Victoria. He won another Welsh League medal in 1895-96 when he was one of nine ever-presents in the Wrexham side.

When the Robins rejoined the Combination League in 1896, Harrison switched to wing-half, although he occasionally appeared in the forward line when the club were short. In 1899 he surprisingly won the first of five Welsh caps when he played against England after the Welsh selectors thought he had been born in Portmadog!

He went on to win Combination League Championship medals in 1901, 1902 and 1903 and though he played the last of his 193 first team games in a 4-1 FA Cup preliminary defeat at home to Rhyl in September 1905, he continued to play for the club's Reserves for a further four years.

On his retirement from the playing side of the game he became a member of the club's Management committee, later becoming a director and a club chairman, a position he held until his death in 1920.

HAT-TRICK HEROES

Wrexham players have netted 98 hat-tricks in Football League games with Tommy Bamford holding the record with 13. He also scored another three in Cup matches.

The club's first hat-trick in the Football League was scored by Ted Regan in the 6-1 win over Chesterfield on 5th November 1921. Bill Cotton also scored three goals in the same match but Regan was to reach the feat first. There have also been two other League games when two Wrexham players have scored hat-tricks in the same match and one Welsh Cup tie. In the League, James Jones and Jack Nock each scored three goals in a 6-2 win over Wigan Borough on 14th March 1925, and Tommy Bannan and Eric Betts netted three goals apiece on 24th October 1953, when Workington were beaten 8-0. In the Welsh Cup competition of 1957-58, Bannan and Barry Smith both scored a hat-trick in a 7-0 win over Flint Town at the Racecourse Ground.

The only occasion when three Wrexham players have scored a hat-trick in the same match occurred on 3rd March 1962, when Wyn Davies, Roy Ambler and Ron Barnes each scored three goals in the 10-1 rout of Hartlepool United.

Although 60 players have scored Football League hat-tricks for the club, it is surprising to find that Arfon Griffiths who scored 120 League goals for the Robins, managed only one hat-trick.

The last hat-trick hero in a League game for the Robins was Karl Connolly against Luton Town at Kenilworth Road on 20th September 1997, when Wrexham ran out winners 5-2.

HEWITT, CHARLIE

Charlie Hewitt began his managerial career with Mold before joining Wrexham in November 1924. Though the team gradually improved under his guidance they never reached higher than 16th but they did win the Welsh Cup in 1925, beating Flint in the final. At the end of the 1925-26 season he left the Racecourse Ground and had spells in charge of Flint and Connah's Quay before joining Chester in 1930.

Hewitt steered them to Football League membership the following year and in six years at Sealand Road he twice led the club to third position. In April 1936, he accepted a lucrative offer to manage Millwall. He revamped the London club on and off the field, making sweeping changes in every department. Success soon came and Millwall became the first Division Three club to reach the FA Cup semifinal where they lost to Sunderland. The following season, the Lions won the Third Division (South) championship but Hewitt was later suspended for making illegal payments to players and he was sacked soon afterwards.

After the war he became manager of Leyton Orient but after two poor seasons he was enticed back to The Den. However, his second period was not as successful as his first and he was sacked in January 1956. He later issued a writ for breach of contract and was awarded £4,500 damages.

HEWITT, RON

Inside-forward Ron Hewitt was a junior with Wolverhampton Wanderers but after failing to make the grade at Molineux, he had a short spell with Walsall in 1949 and then spent 1950 at Darlington. A move to Wrexham in 1951 saw the Flint-born player embark on a six-year stay at the Racecourse Ground.

He played his first match for Wrexham in a 2-1 defeat at Chester on the opening day of the 1951-52 season, a season in which he topped the club's scoring charts with 16 goals in 38 League games. After netting 13 in 1952-53 he topped the club's scoring lists a second time the following season with 15 goals. His best season in terms of goals scored was 1956-57 when he scored 22 goals from just 31 League appearances including hat-tricks against Barrow (Home 5-0) and Carlisle United (Home 6-4). That campaign also saw him represent the Third Division (North) team against the South but in the summer of 1957 he left the Racecourse Ground to join Cardiff City for £7,000.

Within months of his arrival at Ninian Park, Hewitt won his first full Welsh cap when he played against Northern Ireland and went on to make four more appearances for his country including three in the 1958 World Cup Finals in Sweden. He led the Bluebirds' goal charts for two successive seasons which included a hat-trick in a 4-3 home win over Blackburn Rovers in March 1958.

He returned to Wrexham two years after leaving the club and after a further season in which he took his Wrexham goals tally to 111 in 267 first team games, he joined Coventry City for £4,500. He later ended his League career with Chester before playing non-League football for Hereford United, Northwich Victoria, Witton Albion and Caernarfon.

HILL, ALAN

One of Wrexham's most versatile players, Alan Hill made his first team debut as a replacement for the injured Joey Jones in a 1-1 draw at Charlton Athletic in January 1975.

Though he was never a first team regular in his nine seasons at the Racecourse Ground, his ability to play in any position ensured that his was the first name on the manager's lips should anyone be injured or lose form. In 1979-80 he played nine different numbered shirts including the goalkeeper's!

He won a Third Division championship medal in 1977-78 and experienced European football with the Robins, scoring a goal in a 5-2 defeat at FC Magdeburg in October 1979.

When Wrexham entertained Arsenal in the sixth round of the 1977-78 FA Cup competition, Hill beat the Gunners' offside trap but with only the 'keeper to beat, he shot narrowly wide and the Robins lost 3-2.

After the club were relegated to the Fourth Division in 1982-83, Hill, who had appeared in 257 first team games, left the Racecourse Ground to play non-League football for Oswestry Town.

HOME MATCHES

Wrexham's best home win in the Football League is the 10-1 victory over Hartlepool United on 3rd March 1962, when Roy Ambler, Ron Barnes and Wyn Davies all scored hat-tricks.

They have scored 11 goals in home games in other competitions on three occasions, beating Caergwrle 11-1 in the Welsh League in 1894-95; Rhyl 11-0 in the FA Cup in 1911-12 and New Brighton 11-1 in the Football League Northern Section Cup in 1933-34.

HOME SEASONS

Wrexham have gone through a complete League season with an undefeated home record on two occasions – 1966-67 and 1969-70. The club's highest number of home wins in a League season is 18. This was achieved from 21 matches in 1932-33 when the club finished runners-up in the Third Division (North) and in 1952-53 when the club ended the season in third place in Division Three (North).

Barry Horne

HONOURS

The club' major honours are:

Division 3	Champions	1977-78
Division 3	runners-up	1992-93
Division 3 (South)	runners-up	1932-33
Division 4	runners-up	1969-70
Welsh Cup	Winners	1878, 1883, 1893, 1897, 1903, 1905, 1909, 1910, 1911, 1914, 1915, 1921, 1924, 1925, 1931, 1957, 1958, 1960, 1972, 1975, 1978, 1986, 1995

HORNE, BARRY

A late starter to League football, he completed a chemistry degree at Liverpool University while playing as a part-timer for Rhyl in the Northern Premier League. On leaving University he signed for Wrexham who were then in the Fourth Division and made his League debut in a 2-1 defeat at Swindon Town on the opening day of the 1984-85 season. In three years at the Racecourse Ground, Horne won a Welsh Cup winners' medal and impressed in the club's famous European run when he scored one of the goals in the defeat of FC Porto on the away goal rule. After scoring 29 goals in 184 first team games he joined Portsmouth in the summer of 1987.

Within a month of his arrival at Fratton Park, he made his first appearance for the Welsh national side and has since gone on to win 59 caps.

He had made 79 first team appearances for Pompey when Chris Nicholl, Southampton's manager brought him to The Dell for £700,000 – the club's most expensive signing. He quickly settled into the Saints' side and very rarely missed a match. He had played in 144 League and Cup games for the Saints when in July 1992, he was snapped up by Everton. He made 148 first team appearances for the Goodison club before Birmingham City paid £250,000 to secure his services at the end of the 1995-96 season.

HUMES, TONY

Wrexham captain Tony Humes began his Football League career with his home-town club Ipswich Town after working his way through the club's junior ranks. He went on to play in 140 first team games for the

Portman Road club before signing for Wrexham for a fee of £40,000 in March 1992.

The central defender made his debut for the Robins in a 1-1 draw at Chesterfield, going on to play in eight of the nine games that were left. In 1992-93, Humes was ever-present as Wrexham won promotion from the Third Division but in recent seasons his commitment has led to him missing games through both injury and suspension.

One of the club's best buys, Humes has now played in 225 first team games for the Racecourse Ground club and though he has only scored nine goals, they have often proved to be important ones.

HUNDRED GOALS

Wrexham have scored more than 100 League goals in a season on two occasions. They scored 106 goals in 1932-33 when they finished runners-up to Hull City in the Third Division (North) and then the following season scored 102 goals when finishing sixth in the Third Division (North).

I

INGLE, STEVE

Bradford-born Steve Ingle began his career with his home town club Bradford City. After playing in the Valley Parade club's Northern Intermediate and Northern Regional Leagues he made his first team debut against Lincoln City in September 1964, at the age of only 17. This was no mean achievement for a player who had broken his leg twice when playing for Bradford Schoolboys two years earlier.

He had played in 90 League games for the Yorkshire club but was unhappy at being asked to play at centre-forward in the later stages of his Valley Parade career and moved to Southend United. He returned to his more customary role of right-back at Roots Hall but when Southend manager Alvan Williams took charge at the Racecourse Ground, Ingle was persuaded to follow him and signed for the Robins for a fee of £2,000.

He made his debut in a 1-1 home draw against Luton Town on the opening day of the 1967-68 campaign and over the next five seasons proved himself a great crowd favourite. When the club won promotion to the Third Division in 1969-70, Ingle's aggressive runs down the right flank were a prominent feature of the club's play. He went on to appear in 178 first team games before joining Stockport County in the summer of 1972. He only stayed one season at Edgeley Park before playing for Southport and later Darlington.

INTERNATIONAL MATCHES

The Racecourse Ground has been host to quite a number of international matches. The first was in March 1877, when Scotland beat Wales 2-0. The Scots have also inflicted the heaviest defeats on Wales at the Racecourse, winning 8-1 in 1885 and 8-0 in 1893. The biggest win for Wales came in 1888 when Ireland were beaten 11-0. The biggest attendance for an international game at the Racecourse Ground is 33,160 in 1948 when Wales beat Northern Ireland 2-0.

INTERNATIONAL PLAYERS

Wrexham's most capped player (ie: caps gained while players were registered with the club) is Joey Jones with 29 caps. The following is a complete list of players who have gained full international honours for Wales whilst at the Racecourse Ground.

Player	Caps Won	Player	Caps Won
T.Bamford	5	Sam Jones	2
H.E.Blew	22	S.Jones	1
T.H.Boden	1	F.C.Kelly	2
T.Burke	5	A.Lea	4
L.Cartwright	2	B.Lewis	7
T.Carty	1	T.Lewis	2
W.Crompton	3	B.W.Lloyd	3
E.A.Cross	2	J.W.Lloyd	1
A.Davies	2	A.A.Lumberg	3
A.O.Davies	1	A.S.Marriott	2
G.Davies	3	T.J.Mathias	12
Revd H.Davies	1	A.W.Mays	1
James Davies	1	J.T.Morgan	1

John Davies	1	J.Owens	1
L.Davies	4	H.Phoenix	1
O.Davies	1	G.Poland	2
R.Davies	3	D.Powell	1
R.O.Davies	2	I.H.Price	3
Walter Davies	1	J.Price	7
William Davies	2	D.H.Pugh	4
W.D.Davies	28	James Roberts	2
C.dwards	1	R.Roberts	3
R.I.Edwards	1	W.Roberts	4
R.E.Evans	2	J.P.Rogers	3
R.O.Evans	4	W.Rogers	2
J.A.Eyton-Jones	4	H.Sisson	3
R.J.Finnigan	1	D.P.Smallman	3
S.G.Gillam	2	J.Taylor	1
G.W.Glascodine	1	G.Thomas	2
G.A.Godding	2	M.R.Thomas	11
A.T.Griffiths	17	J.Trainer	3
S.L.Griffiths	1	J.H.Turner	1
W.C.Harrison	5	R.E.Turner	2
A.Hayes	2	W.H.Turner	5
T.J.Hewitt	3	J.Wilding	6
E.Hughes	4	A.L.Williams	1
G.P.Jones	2	G.O.Williams	1
J.Jones	1	J.T.Williams	1
J.P.Jones	29	G.A.Wynn	3

Wrexham's first players to be capped were Edwin Cross and Alfred Davies who were both in the Welsh side that played their inaugural fixture against Scotland in 1876.

INVITATION CUP

Wrexham won the FA of Wales Invitation Cup on 17th May 1998, when they beat Cardiff City 2-1.

J

JACKSON, PETER

Born in Luddenden Foot, Peter Jackson began in local football with his home-town club and Hebden Bridge before signing for Stoke in 1924. In his ten years at the club, spanning three divisions, he only made 71 appearances. In 1934 he moved to Southend United but after only three League appearances he returned to the Victoria Ground as assistant to the Potters' manager Bob McGrory. He stayed at Stoke until November 1950, when he was appointed as manager of Wrexham.

His best season at the Racecourse Ground was 1952-53 when the Robins finished in third place in the Third Division (North). In 1954-55 he gave League debuts to his twin sons, David and Peter junior but in February 1955, he left Wrexham to manage Bradford City.

His sons followed him to Valley Parade where brought an air of confidence to the club. In 1957-58 he led the club to third place and into the newly formed Third Division the following season. But after years of struggling, City dropped into the Fourth Division in 1961. Relegation inevitably meant dismissal and after six years, Jackson's reign as Bradford City manager was over.

JONES, ALF

Only Arfon Griffiths has played in more Football League games for Wrexham than Alf Jones. Born in Chester, he played his early football for local junior side Brickfield's before moving to Saltney Athletic.

He joined Wrexham in the summer of 1923 and made his debut in a 4-0 home win over Ashington United on the opening day of the 1923-24 season. That campaign he was the club's only ever-present, an achievement he repeated in seasons 1926-27, 1927-28, 1930-31, 1931-32, 1932-33 and 1933-34.

A model of consistency, Jones played twice played in runs of over 100 consecutive League games – 138 between 3rd October 1925, and 25th December 1928, and 201 between 30th August 1930, and 6th April 1935.

Affectionately known as 'Pride of Wrexham' and 'Our Alf' he was a hard-tackling full-back with good distributional skills. With Wrexham he won three Welsh Cup winners' medals in 1924, 1925 and 1931 and two runners-up medals in 1932 and 1933.

He had appeared in 575 first team games when at the end of the 1935-36 season he was allowed to leave the Racecourse Ground and joined Winsford United in the Cheshire League.

JONES, GREN

A former England Schoolboy and Youth international, Grenville Jones began his career with West Bromwich Albion but after six years at The Hawthorns in which he made only three League appearances, the speedy winger joined Wrexham.

He played his first game for the club in a 3-1 win at York City on the opening day of the 1955-56 season and over the next six years made the Number 7 shirt his own, playing in 281 first team games. Though not a prolific scorer, he netted 43 goals including a hat-trick in a 6-0 home win over Hull City on 28th September 1957. Whilst at the Racecourse Ground he won three Welsh Cup winners' medals and was impressive during the club's fine Football League Cup run of 1960-61.

At the end of that season, Jones left Wrexham to play in Australia for the New South Wales club, Prague, later joining Sydney FC.

JONES, JOEY

A Welsh Youth international, Joey Jones made his Wrexham debut at the age of 17 in a 1-1 draw at Rotherham United in January 1973. The Bangor-born full-back went on to play in 118 first team games before Liverpool's Bob Paisley paid £110,000 for him in July 1975.Signed to replace the out-of-form Alec Lindsay, there were too many rough edges for the top flight and he found himself out of the side. That disappointment however was merely a prelude to his finest season of 1976-77 when he won a European Cup winners' medal and a League Championship medal whilst the Reds narrowly lost the FA Cup Final to Manchester United. Strong and quick, Jones was as tough a full-back as any in the First Division. He had played in 97 games for the Anfield club when in October 1978, he returned to Wrexham for £210,000.

Jones' first season in his second spell at the Racecourse Ground was

Joey Jones

the club's first in the Second Division. He stayed for four years but after the club were relegated in 1981-82 he played in just seven matches the following season before John Neal his former boss at the Racecourse Ground took him to Chelsea.

During his three years at Stamford Bridge, Jones won a Second Division championship medal and made 78 League appearances before moving on to Huddersfield Town. After 68 appearances for the Terriers he returned to North Wales for a third stint with Wrexham.

In his second season back with the Robins he helped them reach the play-off final where they lost to Leyton Orient. In December 1989, Wrexham manager Brian Flynn made him player-coach and after playing the last of his 482 first team games at home to Chesterfield in November 1991, he has since concentrated on coaching.

JONES, PETER

Salford-born defender Peter Jones signed amateur forms for Manchester United but within twelve months had left Old Trafford to join the ground staff at Wolverhampton Wanderers. However, he became homesick at Molineux and after one season, returned to United. After signing part-time professional forms, he made his debut for the Old Trafford club against Portsmouth on 19th October 1957. A former England Youth player, he was a regular in the British Army side before being allowed to leave Old Trafford and join Wrexham in March 1960. He made his debut for the Robins the following month in a 2-0 defeat at Halifax Town but then was a virtual ever-present for the next six seasons, playing in 272 League and Cup games and scoring eight goals.

In 1961-62 he missed just two games as the club won promotion to the Third Division and the following season was the club's only ever-present as they consolidated their position in the higher grade of football. He won two Welsh Cup runners-up medals in 1962 and 1965 but at the end of the 1965-66 season in which Wrexham finished 92nd in the Football League, he left the Racecourse Ground to join Stockport County.

At Edgeley Park he played in 56 first team games before hanging up his boots.

K

KEAY, JACK

Glasgow-born Jack Keay joined Celtic as an apprentice but was later released and joined Shrewsbury Town. He made his debut for the Gay Meadow club as a substitute in a 3-1 defeat at Chesterfield in September 1977, and soon established himself as a first team regular. He won a Third Division championship medal in 1978-79 and was ever-present the following season in the Second Division. He went on to score 23 goals in 195 League and Cup games for Shrewsbury before joining Wrexham for a fee of £18,000 in September 1982.

His first game in Wrexham colours was in a 1-0 home defeat by Lincoln City and though he was a virtual ever-present, he could do nothing to halt the club's slide into the Fourth Division. Having gained two Welsh Cup runners-up medals in 1983 and 1984, he was unfortunate in missing the club's 1986 success over Kidderminster Harriers, having played in all the earlier rounds. Having played in 199 first team games for the Robins he was given a free transfer at the end of the 1985-86 season and joined Irish League club, Derry City. In his first season he helped them win promotion and later the Irish Cup as well as playing in Europe, before becoming the club's player-coach.

KEELAN, KEVIN

Calcutta-born goalkeeper Kevin Keelan signed professional forms for Aston Villa in 1958 and made five first team appearances before joining Stockport County in April 1961. After just three appearances for the Edgeley Park club, he moved into non-League football with Kidderminster Harriers. It was from here that Wrexham manager Ken Barnes signed him in November 1961, and the following month he made his debut for the Robins in a 4-2 win at Colchester United. He went on to appear in 24 League games that season as the club won promotion to the Third Division. A great crowd favourite, he missed just two games in the 1962-63 campaign but in the close season he joined Norwich City for a fee of £6,500.

After making his Norwich debut against Cardiff City in August 1963, Kevin Keelan stayed at Carrow Road until February 1980, mak-

Kevin Keelan

ing 673 first team appearances. He helped the Canaries to the First Division twice, played in two League Cup Finals and was a League ever-present in five seasons.

KINSEY, ALBERT

A former England Schoolboy, Albert Kinsey began his career with Manchester United but after working through the club's junior teams, he made just one first team appearance in a 2-1 win for United against Chester in a third round FA Cup match.

After that he returned to the club's Central League side before joining Wrexham in March 1966.

Over the next seven seasons, Kinsey was a regular in the Robins' side, with his best season being 1969-70 when he helped the club win promotion to the Third Division. In that campaign, he was Wrexham's only ever-present and the leading goal-scorer in the Fourth Division with 27 League goals. Included in that total were hat-tricks against York City (Home 4-0) and Bradford (Home 4-0). He topped the club's scoring charts in 1970-71 and 1971-72 and in this second season scored the winner in the Welsh Cup final against Cardiff City. The following season he scored the club's first-ever goal in Europe in a 1-1 draw against FC Zurich. In March 1973, he moved to Crewe Alexandra and after making 32 League appearances joined non-League Wigan Athletic.

One of the club's most popular players, he scored 98 goals in 297 games for the Robins.

L

LAPHAM, HAROLD

After beginning his footballing career with non-League Marine, Liverpool-born Harold Lapham joined Blackburn Rovers as an amateur in November 1934. His impressive form in the Ewood Park club's reserve side led to him being given a professional contract but eight months later he was given a free transfer and joined Accrington Stanley. After making seven League appearances for the Peel Park club in which he scored two goals, he joined Wrexham in the summer of 1936.

He made a goal-scoring debut in a 6-2 defeat at Lincoln City and in fact, scored in each of his first four games for the club, the other three all being won. He ended that 1936-37 season as the club's top scorer with 22 League goals, including four in a 6-0 home win over Gateshead. He also topped the club's scoring chart the following season with 16 goals in 32 appearances including a hat-trick in a 6-3 win over Hartlepool United at the Racecourse Ground.

He had scored 41 goals in 73 League and Cup games for the Robins when he left the club at the end of the 1938-39 season.

LARGEST CROWD

It was on 26th January 1957, that the Racecourse Ground housed its largest crowd. The occasion was the FA Cup fourth round match against Manchester United. A crowd of 34,445 saw the Robins lose 5-0.

LATE FINISHES

Wrexham's final match of the season against Tranmere Rovers at the Racecourse Ground on 14th June 1947, is the latest date for the finish of any Robins' season. A crowd of 2,913 turned up to see the two sides play out a goal-less draw in the Third Division (North) encounter.

LEA, ARTHUR

Though he only had one arm, Arthur Lea was noted for his powerful kicking and first played for the club in a 4-1 defeat at Chirk on 29th November 1884. In 1889 he won the first of four Welsh caps when he played against England and in 1893 he captained his country in the match against Northern Ireland in Belfast.

One of the highlights of Lea's career was when he captained the Wrexham side that bat Chirk 2-1 to win the Welsh Cup in 1893. He also gained runners-up medals in the competition in 1890, 1891 and 1895.

When the club entered the Combination League in season 1890-91, it was Lea who scored the club's first goal in the competition in a 5-1 defeat at Gorton Villa.

Shortly after playing in his fourth international match for Wales he became very ill and almost lost a leg. He recovered to play some games during the 1894-95 campaign but after scoring 33 goals in 112 appearances including a hat-trick in a 10-0 win over Denton in 1891-92 he decided to hang up his boots.

LEADING SCORERS

Wrexham have provided the Football League's leading divisional goal-scorer on two occasions. In 1969-70, Albert Kinsey scored 27 goals to head the Fourth Division charts and in 1994-95, Gary Bennett netted 29 goals to top the Third Division charts.

LEAGUE GOALS – CAREER HIGHEST

Tommy Bamford holds the Racecourse Ground record for the most League goals with a career total of 174 between 1929 and 1935.

LEAGUE GOALS – LEAST CONCEDED

During the 1978-79 season, Wrexham conceded just 42 goals but could still only finish 15th in the Second Division following their promotion as champions of Division Three the previous season.

LEAGUE GOALS – MOST CONCEDED

Wrexham conceded 107 goals during the 1963-64 season including nine at Brentford. Not surprisingly they finished 23rd in the Third Division and were relegated to the Fourth Division.

LEAGUE GOALS – MOST INDIVIDUAL

Tommy Bamford holds the Wrexham record for the most League goals in a season with 44 scored in the Third Division (North) during the 1933-34 season.

LEAGUE GOALS – MOST SCORED

Wrexham's highest goals tally in the Football League was during the 1932-33 Third Division (North) season when they scored 106 goals in finishing runners-up to Hull City.

LEAGUE VICTORY – HIGHEST

Wrexham's best League victory was the 10-1 win over Hartlepool United at the Racecourse Ground on 3rd March 1962. Three players scored hat-tricks in the match, Wyn Davies, Roy Ambler and Ron Barnes with Stan Bennion scoring the other goal.

LEE STUART

Stuart Lee joined Bolton Wanderers straight from school and after progressing through the junior ranks, made his first team debut in a goal-less draw at York City on New Year's Day 1972. In 1972-73 he became a regular in the side as Bolton won the Third Division championship and scored his first hat-trick in a 3-0 win over Halifax Town.

Stuart Lee

Finding life in the Second Division a little tougher, he left Burnden Park after scoring 27 goals in 101 League and Cup games to join Wrexham in November 1975, for a club record fee of £15,000.

He scored from the penalty spot on his debut in a 1-1 home draw against Halifax and netted four goals in an 8-0 Welsh Cup victory over Llandiloes. Also in that 1975-76 season, he played in two European Cup Winners' Cup matches and scored the Wrexhm goal in the quarter-final match against Anderlecht.

He had scored 20

goals in 71 first team matches for the Robins when he was given a free transfer and joined Stockport County. At Edgeley Park he enjoyed his most consistent season, missing just one game in the 1978-79 season and was the club's top scorer with 24 goals.

In September 1979, Manchester City signed him for £60,000 but he played only six times in the First Division, scoring twice. His contract was cancelled six months later and he went to play in the NASL for Portland Timbers and Tampa Bay Rowdies.

LEWIS, BEN

Ben Lewis started his career with Chester, where he won the first of ten Welsh international caps when he played against Ireland in Belfast in 1891. In the summer of that year he joined Wrexham but spent only one season with the Welsh club, netting a hat-trick in a 3-1 win at Stockport County before signing for Middlesbrough.

After only one season in the north-east, he returned to the Racecourse Ground and over the next two seasons, scored 26 goals in 49 games including hat-tricks against Westminster (Home 4-0) and Macclesfield Town (Home 7-1), the latter match being in the FA Cup competition of 1894-95. That season he was one of three ever-presents as Wrexham were crowned champions of the Welsh League.

However, at the end of the season, Lewis decided he wanted to play in a higher standard of football and so returned to Chester. But in 1896 upon Wrexham's return to the Combination League, Lewis signed for the club for a third time. In 1896-97 he won a Welsh Cup winners' medal and the following season, a runners-up medal in the same competition. When the club reached the Welsh Cup Final again in 1898-99, Lewis was surprisingly omitted on the eve of the replay which Wrexham lost 1-0 to Druids.

Lewis immediately severed all connections with the club and played for Buckley Victoria in the Welsh League for one season before retiring in 1901.

LEYLAND DAF CUP

The Leyland Daf Cup replaced the Sherpa Van Trophy for the 1989-90 season. Wrexham's opening match of the preliminary round saw them beat Blackpool 1-0 with Graham Cooper grabbing the all-important goal but they then went to Gigg Lane and were beaten 4-1 by Bury with Gary Worthington netting for the Robins from the penalty-spot.

Despite not winning any of their group games in 1990-91, drawing 3-3 at home to Peterborough United and losing 1-0 at Cambridge United, the Robins won through to the knockout stages where they played Brentford at Griffin Park. After extra-time the game was still goal-less and went to penalties with Brentford winning 3-0.

LLOYD, BRIAN

After beginning his career with Rhyl, goalkeeper Brian Lloyd joined Stockport County for a fee of £1,000. After two seasons of sharing the

goalkeeping duties with Alan Ogley, he left Edgeley Park and joined Southend United for £10,000. He was never happy in his two year spell at Roots Hall and was quick to take the opportunity to return to North Wales when Wrexham offered to buy him.

After making his debut in a 2-1 defeat at Blackburn Rovers in August 1971, he shared the number one shirt with David Gaskell until 4th March 1972, when he embarked upon a remarkable run, playing in every game until his last appearance on 20th August 1977. This run consisted of 248 League

Brian Lloyd

matches and a record 312 appearances in all competitions. His successful period in the Robins team of the 1970s was further boosted by his selection for the full Welsh international side, for whom he won three caps Following the appointment of Arfon Griffiths as manager, Lloyd was dropped and in September 1977, he moved to Chester.

He made 94 League appearances for the then Sealand Road club and had a loan spell at Port vale before returning to Stockport County for a second stint. During this spell, Lloyd became the only County goalkeeper to score a League goal when with a gale force wind behind him he netted at Bradford City. At the beginning of the 1982-83 season, Lloyd completed his 500th League appearance but at the end of that campaign, he retired at the age of 35.

LLOYD, CLIFF

Cliff Lloyd served Wrexham Football Club as a player, secretary and manager for 41 years.

He played his early football for his home-town club, Brymbo before joining Wrexham in 1932 as an amateur. He turned professional four years later but didn't make his League debut until March 1938, when he played in a 2-1 home win over Rochdale. He went on to make 12 League appearances for the Robins, scoring two goals. During the war years, Lloyd played 51 games but when the fighting ended he became assistant-secretary at the Racecourse Ground before taking over the full secretarial duties upon the appointment of Les McDowall in May 1949. Following McDowall's departure, Lloyd became caretaker-manager until Peter Jackson took over the reins in November 1950, and he reverted to his secretarial duties.

When Jackson left the Racecourse Ground in February 1955, Lloyd was appointed manager. The Robins were then at the foot of the Third Division (North) but Lloyd led them to 18th place and in 1955-56 they were 14th. The following season, they moved up to 12th place, won the Welsh Cup and reached the fourth round of the FA Cup. Lloyd discovered a number of fine players,. including Wyn Davies and Arfon Griffiths but in October 1957, he resigned as manager. After that he was caretaker-manager on a further three occasions, whilst still continuing his secretarial duties.

Cliff Lloyd retired in 1973, but sadly his retirement was short-lived for in June of that year, the former Denbighshire cricketer collapsed and died whilst batting for Brymbo in a cup match, aged only 56.

LOAN PLAYERS

Though Wrexham have taken a number of players on loan over the years, the first was the former Crystal Palace youth captain, Tommy Vansittart. He arrived at the Racecourse Ground in February 1970, to strengthen a Wrexham team that won promotion to the Third Division at the end of the season. He made his debut in a 1-0 defeat at Exeter City on St Valentine's Day and signed on a permanent basis at the end of that promotion-winning season. Hampered by injuries, especially a broken leg, he was forced to give the game up after 99 first team appearances for the Robins.

LOGAN, JAMES

A Scottish Junior international, he began his League career with Bradford City, where his brother Peter appeared in well over 300 games. He then joined Chesterfield and later played for Bradford Park Avenue before returning to Scotland to manage Raith Rovers.

In 1921-22 they finished third behind Celtic and Rangers in the Scottish First Division and in ten years with the Stark's Park club, he produced some fine players, notably Alex James who was sold to Preston North End for £3,250. After running a pub in Kerriemuir, he was appointed Wrexham manager in January 1937.

During that first season, Wrexham did quite well, reaching the third round of the FA Cup and finishing eighth in the Third Division (North). The following season they finished tenth but with one game of the 1937-38 season still to play, he resigned agreeing to take charge for the last match against Hartlepool United which was lost 2-0.

LONGMUIR, ARCHIE

Archie Longmuir began his career with Glasgow Celtic but after failing to make a first team appearance he came south of the border to join Blackburn Rovers. After 18 months at Ewood Park, in which he made 20 League appearances, scoring twice, he moved to Rovers' Lancashire neighbours, Oldham Athletic. In 1923-24 he appeared in

22 League games for the Latics but at the end of the season he left to sign for Wrexham.

He made his debut in a 3-1 reversal at Halifax Town on the opening day of the 1924-25 season and over the next six seasons, was a virtual ever-present, only missing odd games due to injury.

One of the game's best wingers, his speed caused many a problem for the opposing full-backs, who often resorted to fouling the clever Longmuir. Though not a prolific scorer, he netted 39 goals in 254 League and Cup appearances with a best of 12 in 41 League games in 1928-29 when the club finished third in Division Three (North).

Towards the end of the following season, he lost his place to Albert Williams and decided to hang up his boots.

LONG SERVICE

One of the club's most illustrious personalities, Ted Robinson served Wrexham for 50 years. He joined them just before the start of the 1893-94 season and after a term of reserve football he made his first team debut against Caergwrle Wanderers in a Welsh League fixture on 27th October 1894. He went on to captain the club to four Combination League titles and to victory in three Welsh Cup finals. After appearing in 297 games he became club secretary and though he retired in 1929 he returned shortly afterwards as financial secretary, following Jack Baynes' poor health and held that position until he retired in 1943.

LOVE, JOHN

He played his early football with Leith Athletic before moving into the Scottish League with Hibernian. Like many others, his career was interrupted by the Second World War when he served as a flight-lieutenant with Bomber Command and then as a glider pilot. He was awarded the DFC after he was wounded by shrapnel during the crossing of the Rhine in 1944.

When peacetime football resumed, he rejoined Leith Athletic before signing for Albion Rovers, whom he helped win promotion to the Scottish League First Division.

In 1949 he moved south of the border to play for Nottingham Forest and in 1950-51 helped them win the Third Division (South) championship. After scoring 21 goals in 59 games for Forest, he surprisingly left the City Ground to play non-League football for Llanelli, whom he also managed.

Love returned to the League scene with Walsall in March 1955, as player-assistant manager to Major Frank Buckley. A few weeks later, Buckley resigned and Love took over until December 1957, when he moved to Wrexham as manager. The Robins finished 12th that season and so just managed to get into the newly-formed Third Division in 1958. The following season they finished 18th but after the club had won only five of their first 20 games in 1959-60, he resigned.

LOWEST

The lowest number of goals scored by Wrexham in a single Football League season is 37 in 1923-24. The club's lowest points record in the Football League occurred in seasons 1925-26, 1949-50 and 1963-64 when they gained just 32 points.

LUMBERG, ALBERT

Full-back Albert Lumberg played his early football with Connah's Quay, Shotton and Mold before following the latter club's manager Charlie Hewitt to the Racecourse Ground.

He made his League debut for Wrexham in a 3-0 defeat at Chesterfield on New Year's Day and soon established himself as a first team regular. Forming a successful full-back partnership with Alf Jones, his performances led to him winning the first of three Welsh caps against Ireland in 1929. He had played in 178 League and Cup games for the Robins when in May 1930, he was allowed to leave the Racecourse Ground and join Wolverhampton wanderers for a fee of £650. Despite spending three seasons at Molineux he could never guarantee himself a first team place and in the summer of 1933 he joined Brighton and Hove Albion. After one season he returned to the north-west to play for Stockport County but after only two appearances he signed for Clapton Orient.

Unable to break into the first team, he had a short spell with non-League Lytham before returning to League action with New Brighton. He later played a number of games for Winsford United before becoming player-manager of Newry Town.

M

McDOWALL, LES

Les McDowall was born in India, the son of a Scottish missionary. He trained as a draughtsman but was made unemployed from his shipyard in the early 1930s. Along with a number of others in the same position, they formed a football team, Glentyon Thistle and while playing for this side he was spotted by Sunderland and signed for them on Christmas Eve 1932. In over five years at Roker Park, he made only 13 appearances and in March 1938, Manchester City paid £7,000 for his services.

He took over the captaincy in 1938-39 but then the war disrupted his career. When League football resumed in 1946, McDowall was still a regular in the half-back line and although no longer captain, he helped them win the Second Division title in 1946-47.

In June 1949, he took over as player-manager of Wrexham but selected himself just three times before hanging up his boots to concentrate on management. After less than a year at the Racecourse Ground, in which the team struggled, he was offered a return to City when manager Jock Thomson decided to leave football. Just as his arrival as a player at Maine Road coincided with relegation to Division Two, so his ascension to manager at City came as the club dropped out of Division One. In his first season he got the club back to the top flight and they remained there until the last of his 13 years at the helm. He enjoyed a measure of success in the FA Cup, losing to Newcastle United in the 1955 final and beating Birmingham City the year after. To have lasted so long at Maine Road with little to show in terms of League honours suggests the confidence the club had in him.

McGOWAN, ALY

Full-back Aly McGowan began his career with Scottish League St Johnstone but after two seasons with the Perth club in which he was capped by Scotland at 'B' level, he was surprisingly given a free transfer and joined Wrexham.

After playing his first game in a 1-1 home draw against Crewe Alexandra on the opening day of the 1953-54 season, he went on to give the Welsh club ten seasons of loyal service before breaking a leg.

With Wrexham he helped the club win promotion to the Third Division in 1961-62 and won three Welsh Cup winners' medals in 1957, 1958 and 1960.

It was on 13th April 1963, that McGowan broke his leg in a goalless home draw against Watford but though he made a comeback at Darlington on 5th April 1965, it proved to be his last and 478th appearance in a Wrexham shirt.

He was awarded a testimonial match against Chester and took charge of the club's 'A' team before spending seven years looking after the Northern Floodlit League side and combining it with the duties of groundsman at the Racecourse Ground.

McMILLAN, SAMMY

Belfast-born Sammy McMillan was only 14 when he played for Ards Reserves. However, though he later signed for Linfield, it was whilst with Boyland Boys Club that he was spotted by Manchester United scouts and joined their ground staff at the age of 16. He eventually made his United debut in a side still rebuilding after the Munich air disaster and in that first season, scored six goals in 11 games. Capped twice by Northern Ireland, he left Old Trafford in December 1963, to join Wrexham for a fee of £8,000.

He played his first game for the Robins in a 3-2 home defeat by Shrewsbury Town, two days later scoring the winning goal in a 2-1 win for Wrexham at Gay Meadow. Though these were generally dark days for the Welsh club, McMillan went on to score 62 goals in 172 League and Cup games after the winger had been converted first to an inside-forward and then a wing-half. He netted his first hat-trick for the club in a 4-0 home win over Aldershot on 2nd October 1965, and the following season was the club's top scorer with 22 League and Cup goals, including another hat-trick in a 6-0 defeat of Bradford.

In September 1967, he moved to Southend United but after making 77 League appearances in which he scored five goals, he joined Chester. He was hampered by injuries at Sealand Road and in the summer of 1970 he signed for Stockport County. Though he only stayed for two seasons at Edgeley Park, he was the club's top scorer in each of them, having to quit the game prematurely because of a back injury.

McNEIL, DIXIE

A much travelled goal-scorer, Dixie McNeil began his career with Leicester City but having failed to make the Filbert Street club's League side, he joined Exeter City in the summer of 1966. After playing in 31 games for the Grecians, he dropped down to the Southern League with Corby Town, but Northampton Town saw his potential and he responded with 33 goals in 86 League games. In January 1972, he joined Lincoln City and after scoring 53 goals in 97 League games, signed for the League's newest club, Hereford United.

His 34 goals in 1975-76 helped the Edgar Street club win the Third Division championship but after just one season in the Second Division they were relegated and McNeil who had scored 85 goals in 129 League games for Hereford joined Wrexham for a fee of £65,000.

In 1977-78, McNeil scored 13 goals in 23 games as the Robins won the Third Division championship and scored in every round of the FA Cup, a total of 11 goals as Wrexham reached the sixth round for the second time in their history. He went on to score 88 goals in 222 games for the Racecourse club before returning to Hereford United in October 1982.

Dixie McNeil

After only a dozen appearances he returned to the Wrexham area to concentrate on his business interests, but in May 1985, he became Wrexham manager after the club relieved Bobby Roberts of his duties.

His best season in charge at the Racecourse Ground was 1988-89 when the Robins finished fourth and entered the Division Four play-offs. They lost 2-1 on aggregate to Leyton Orient in the final and after a poor start the following season, he resigned.

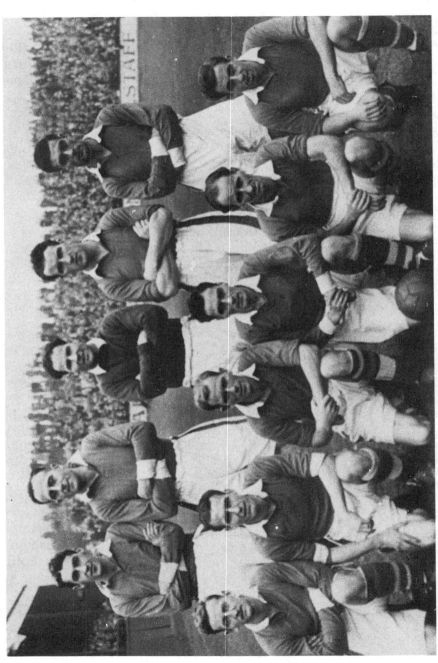

The team for 1946-47

MANAGERS

The following is a complete list of Wrexham's full-time managers together with the inclusive dates for which they held office. Biographies of all the managers of the club are included in alphabetical order elsewhere in this A-Z.

Charlie Hewitt	1924-1926	Billy Morris	1960-1961
Jack Baynes	1929-1931	Ken Barnes	1961-1965
Ernest Blackburn	1932-1937	Billy Morris	1965
James Logan	1937-1938	Jack Rowley	1966-1967
Arthur Cowell	1938	Alvan Williams	1967-1968
Tom Morgan	1939-1942	John Neal	1968-1977
Tom Williams	1942-1949	Arfon Griffiths	1977-1981
Les McDowall	1949-1950	Mel Sutton	1981-1982
Peter Jackson	1950-1955	Bobby Roberts	1982-1985
Cliff Lloyd	1955-1957	Dixie McNeil	1985-1989
John Love	1957-1959	Brian Flynn	1989-

MARATHON MATCHES

Wrexham have been involved in a number of cup games that have gone to three matches. These were: Royal Welsh Warehouse (Welsh Cup 1901-02); Wellington Town (FA Cup 1912-13); Pontypridd (Welsh Cup 1913-14);New Brighton (FA Cup 1926-27); Lincoln City (FA Cup 1946-47); Brighton and Hove Albion (FA Cup 1953-54); Cardiff City (League Cup 1963-64); Aston Villa (League Cup 1971-72); Mansfield Town (FA Cup 1975-76); West Ham United (FA Cup 1980-81) and Chelsea (FA Cup 1981-82).

MARKSMEN – LEAGUE

Wrexham's top League goal-scorer is Tommy Bamford who, struck 174 league goals during his six seasons at the Racecourse Ground. Only two players have hit more than 100 league goals for the club

1.	Tommy Bamford	174
2.	Arfon Griffiths	120
3.	Ron Hewitt	94
4.	Graham Whittle	91
5.	Albert Kinsey	84

6.	Tommy Bannan	83
7.	Gary Bennett	82
8.	Billy Tunnicliffe	74
9.	Billy Ashcroft	72
10.	Karl Connolly	67

MARKSMEN – OVERALL

Only six players have hit a century of goals for Wrexham. The club's top marksman is Tommy Bamford. The Century Club consists of:

1.	Tommy Bamford	207
2.	Arfon Griffiths	141
3.	Graham Whittle	116
4.	Ron Hewitt	111
5.	Gary Bennett	103
6.	Tommy Bannan	100

MARRIOTT, ANDY

An England Youth international goalkeeper, Andy Marriott began his career at Arsenal before Brian Clough paid £50,000 to bring him to Nottingham Forest. Initially he was unable to break into the Forest team and had loan spells with West Bromwich Albion, Blackburn Rovers, Colchester United and Burnley. He spent three months on loan at Turf Moor and won a championship medal as the Clarets won the 1991-92 Fourth Division title.

Eventually he made the breakthrough at the City Ground, albeit because of disciplinary action taken against Forest's regular 'keeper Mark Crossley. He also appeared at Wembley twice, picking up a Zenith Data Systems Cup winners' medal and a League Cup runners-up medal. However, following Forest's relegation from the Premier League in 1993, Marriott found himself out on loan again, this time at Wrexham and he eventually signed for the Welsh club in December 1993, for £200,000.

He had made his debut two months earlier in a 1-1 home draw against Cambridge United and has since been an automatic choice at the Racecourse Ground. In 1995 he won a Welsh Cup winners' medal when Wrexham defeated Cardiff City 2-1 in the final at the Welsh National Stadium.

Although he had previously won International honours for England at Schoolboy, Youth and Under-21 level, it was Wales who handed him his first full cap when he came on during a 2-0 defeat against Switzerland in Lugano in April 1996.

The Sutton-in-Ashfield-born 'keeper didn't miss a League game until 2nd November 1996, having played in 143 consecutive games from his debut. A superb shot stopper, Marriott has now played in 266 League and Cup games for the Welsh club.

Andy Marriott

MASON, STUART

Despite being wanted by both Shrewsbury Town and Wolverhampton Wanderers, right-back Stuart Mason, who was an England Youth international joined Wrexham. He made his debut as a 17-year-old in a 2-0 win at Lincoln City on New Year's Day 1966 and was soon a first team regular in the Robins' side. After playing in the first nine matches of the 1966-67 season, he and Peter Wall were transferred to Liverpool for a combined fee of £30,000.

At Anfield, Mason had two seasons in the club's Central League side and had a lóan spell with Doncaster Rovers before rejoining the Racecourse Ground club in the summer of 1968. For the next five seasons he was a virtual ever-present in the Wrexham side and in 1969-70 helped the club to promotion as they finished runners-up in the Fourth Division. Also during this spell he won a Welsh Cup winners' medal in 1972 and starred in the club's inaugural match in Europe, a 1-1 draw at FC Zurich.

In 1973 he moved to Chester and appeared in 137 League games for the then Sealand Road club as well as having loan spells with Rochdale and Crewe. He then entered non-League football with Bangor City and played for them in the Welsh Cup Final of 1978 against Wrexham.

MATHIAS, TOMMY

A player who always combined playing football with work as a coalminer, he played for Shrewsbury Town in the Birmingham and District League in 1910 and had a season with Chester before joining Wrexham for the start of the 1912-13 season. He made his debut in a 3-0 win over Wolverhampton Wanderers Reserves on the opening day of the season and was one of four ever-presents as Wrexham ended the campaign in sixth place in the Birmingham and District League.

Mathias missed very few games over the next ten seasons, separated by the First World War. In 1914 he won the first of 12 Welsh caps when he played against Scotland and won the last against the same country nine years later.

He won four Welsh Cup winners' medals in 1914, 1915, 1921 and 1925 and played in the club's inaugural game in the Football League against Hartlepool United. He also scored the club's first penalty in the Football League in a 3-1 defeat of Lincoln City on 24th September 1921.

In 1927-28 after he had appeared in 390 League and Cup games for the Robins, he stepped down to play in the club's reserve side to share his experience with the younger players. He later scouted for the Racecourse Ground club before emigrating to Australia in 1964.

MAY, EDDIE

Eddie May started his career as a centre-forward with Athenian League club Dagenham before a switch to full-back alerted Southend United manager Ted Fenton, who offered him a chance with the Roots Hall club. It was the former West Ham boss who moved May to centre-half and he went on to appear in 111 League games for Southend before joining Wrexham for £5,000 in the summer of 1968.

He made his League debut for the Robins in a 2-1 defeat at Aldershot on the opening day of the 1968-69 season and missed just one game that campaign as the club finished ninth in Division Four. Over the next eight seasons he

Eddie May

missed very few games, being ever-present in seasons 1971-72 and 1975-76.

During the club's promotion-winning season of 1969-70, May scored seven League goals from his position at centre-half. It was his best return – the Robins being undefeated whenever he scored!

Captain for most of his time at the Racecourse Ground, he led the Robins to the sixth round of the FA Cup in 1973-74 and to the quarter-finals of the European Cup Winners' Cup in 1975-76. At the end of that season, May who had played in 410 first team games, scoring 44 goals, joined Swansea City on a free transfer.

He made 90 League appearances for the Vetch Field club before taking up coaching posts with Leicester City and Charlton Athletic. After managing Newport County who had just lost their League status, he was in charge of Cardiff City from 1991 to 1994 before becoming boss of Torquay United.

MAYS, ALBERT

Albert Mays began his Football League career with Bristol City and in three seasons with the Ashton Gate club, he scored four goals in 19 games. After moving to Plymouth Argyle in the summer of 1926 he failed to make the first team and after a season joined Merthyr Town. He scored 14 goals in 34 League games for Merthyr before signing for Wrexham in August 1928.

He had a most remarkable debut, scoring all Wrexham's goals in a 4-3 home win over Chesterfield on the opening day of the 1928-29 season. He went on to become the club's top scorer with 32 goals in 34 League games including another four goals in a 5-0 home win over Barrow and a hat-trick in a 4-0 defeat of Ashington, also at the Racecourse Ground.

In 1929 he scored on his debut for Wales against Northern Ireland but was never chosen again.

He had scored 46 goals in 60 League and Cup games for Wrexham when he was transferred to Notts. County in March 1930. He later played for Burnley, Walsall and Halifax Town before ending his playing career with non-League Margate Town.

METCALF, MICKEY

A former Everton Youth player, he joined Wrexham in the summer of 1956 and after impressing in the club's Cheshire League side, made his first team debut at inside-forward in a 3-1 home win over Hartlepool United in October 1957. However, though he kept his place for the following game at Bradford, it was his last first team appearance for two years. On his return to the side on 28th October 1959, he scored both Wrexham goals in a 3-2 home defeat by Chesterfield but even then he only played in four games.

When Ken Barnes was appointed manager, Metcalf was given a regular first team spot and in 1960-61 was the club's top scorer with 22 League and Cup goals including a superb hat-trick in the 3-1 defeat of Blackburn Rovers, the previous season's FA Cup finalists. He was the club's leading scorer again in 1961-62 with 20 goals including his first League hat-trick for the Robins in a 3-1 home win over Doncaster Rovers as they went on to win promotion to the Third Division.

After scoring 73 goals in 145 games for Wrexham he left the Racecourse Ground to continue his career with Chester, where he scored 68 goals in 221 appearances.

METHYLATED SPIRITS

Wrexham defender Wayne Cegielski picked up a useful tip while he was playing with Schalke 04 in Germany. To prevent snow clogging up the boots, the soles were dabbed in methylated spirit. The ball was similarly treated. Wrexham tried it in an FA Cup third round tie on 1st February 1979, against Stockport County and won 6-2 with Wayne Cegielski among the goal-scorers!

MOIR, IAN

Aberdeen-born wing-forward Ian Moir began his career with Manchester United and made his League debut for the Old Trafford club in a 1-1 draw at Bolton Wanderers in October 1960. He went on to score five goals in 45 League games for the Reds over a period of five years before joining Blackpool in February 1965, for £15,000.

At Bloomfield Road he found himself competing with Leslie Lea but when he did play, he forged a rewarding right-wing partnership with Alan Ball. However, at the end of the 1966-67 relegation season,

Ian Moir

Stanley Mortensen began his rebuilding process and sold Moir to Chester City for just over £10,000.

He moved to Wrexham in January 1968, for a similar fee and made his debut in a 2-1 home win over Swansea Town. Moir had excellent ball skills and could beat his man with ease. In 1969-70 he helped the Robins win promotion to the Third Division but he was surprisingly released to Shrewsbury Town in March 1972. Sixteen months later he returned to the Racecourse Ground and played the last of his 199 first team games against Chesterfield in April 1975, before going to play in South Africa.

MORGAN, TOM

Unable to win a regular place in the Port Vale side, he was forced to retire through an injury in 1911. He then joined the club's administrative staff, acting as a scout, as the assistant secretary and as the club's reserve team manager before being appointed as the first-ever Port Vale team manager in October 1929.

In his first season in charge, he guided Vale to the Third Division (North) championship with 67 points and scoring 103 goals. In 1930-31 he guided Vale to fifth in the Second Division – their highest-ever position. However, in the summer of 1932 he was relieved of his post and reverted to the role of assistant-secretary before being promoted to the secretary-manager in December 1937.

He left Vale Park in April 1939, to become secretary-manager of Wrexham. After losing his first two matches in charge, the Robins won three and drew one of their last four matches to finish 14th. After only three games of the 1939-40 season, the Football League was suspended following the declaration of war. He continued to manage the club until March 1942, when he resigned. During his time at the Racecourse Ground, all the club's records were destroyed in a fire at his home.

MORRIS, BILLY

Billy Morris joined Burnley from Llandudno Town in January 1939, and went straight into the Clarets' first team for the match against Norwich City. He had just established himself in the Turf Moor club's side when war was declared. He was a sergeant in the Army during the war, serving in Burma and India.

He gained his first cap for Wales in April 1947, against Scotland and appeared in the 1947 FA Cup Final for Burnley in their 1-0 defeat by Charlton Athletic. He went on to make 230 appearances, scoring 53 goals for the club before retiring in 1952.

After playing non-League football in Wales, he returned to Turf Moor as coach but in the summer of 1960 he was appointed manager of Wrexham.

The Robins had been relegated the previous season and in 1960-61 their first season in the Fourth Division, they finished 16th.

In the summer he was replaced by Ken Barnes but returned to the Racecourse Ground in March 1965, to replace the man who had replaced him! This second spell only lasted seven months in which the club finished 14th in the Fourth Division and reached the Welsh Cup Final where they lost to Cardiff City. After winning only three of the opening 14 matches of the 1965-66 season, Morris was relieved of his duties and replaced by Cliff Lloyd on a caretaker basis until Jack Rowley was appointed in January 1966.

The team for 1975-76

MOST GOALS IN A SEASON

When Wrexham finished the 1932-33 season as runners-up in the Third Division (North) they scored 106 goals in 42 matches. They beat Hartlepool United 8-1, Crewe Alexandra 7-0 and Southport 6-0 and scored five goals in each of four home games against Halifax Town (5-2); New Brighton (5-0); Gateshead (5-1) and Rotherham United (5-1).

MOST MATCHES

Wrexham played their most number of matches, 66, in the 1977-78 season. This comprised of 46 League games, nine FA Cup games, six

League Cup games and five Welsh Cup games, when they won the trophy.

N

NEAL, JOHN

Signed for Hull City by Raich Carter, John Neal played in 60 League games for the Tigers before signing for Swindon Town in July 1957. Two years later, he left the County Ground for Aston Villa and after missing the opening match of the 1959-60 season, played in all the remaining games, winning a Second Division championship medal. He also won a League Cup winners' tankard in 1961 but a year later he left Villa Park after playing in 114 League and Cup games to join Southend United.

After his playing days were over he moved to the Racecourse Ground as first team trainer but when Alvan Williams resigned in September 1968, Neal replaced him. In his first season with the club they finished ninth in the Fourth Division but in 1969-70 he led them to promotion as runners-up to Chesterfield. In 1972 the Robins won the Welsh Cup for the first time in 12 years and in 1973-74 he took the club into the sixth round of the FA Cup for the first time in their history. He led the club to another Welsh Cup victory in 1975 but perhaps his best performance as Wrexham manager was to lead the club into the quarter-finals of the European Cup Winners' Cup in 1976. In 1976-77 he almost took the club into the Second Division for the first time in their history but they lost their last two home matches of the season when a draw with Crystal Palace would have ensured promotion for the club.

He left the Racecourse Ground in May 1977, to take charge at Middlesbrough but left their four years later after a disagreement over the sale of Craig Johnston to Liverpool. He then joined Chelsea and in 1983-84 he took the Stamford Bridge club to the Second Division championship. The following season, the Pensioners were fifth in the First Division and reached the semi-finals of the League Cup but he was still replaced by John Hollins and moved 'upstairs' as a member of the board.

NEUTRAL GROUNDS

The Racecourse Ground has been used as a neutral ground for Welsh Cup Finals on a number of occasions and as early as 5th March 1877, staged an international match between Wales and Scotland. The first Welsh Cup Final to be played at the Racecourse was on 13th March 1880, when the Druids beat Ruthin 2-1. Since that first match against Scotland, over 100 internationals including 'B' Under-23 and Under-21 games have been played at the Racecourse Ground.

The ground has also housed two of Borough United's European Cup Winners' Cup ties in 1963 and Linfield's games in the UEFA Cup of 1988 and European Cup Winners' Cup of 1989.

Wrexham themselves have had to replay on a neutral ground a number of times.

Date	Opponents	Competition	Venue	Score
06.12.1926	New Brighton	FA Cup Rd 1	Anfield	3-1
23.12.1946	Lincoln City	FA Cup Rd 2	Maine Road	1-2
21.12.1953	Brighton HA	FA Cup Rd 2	Selhurst Park	3-1
31.08.1971	Aston Villa	Lg Cup Rd 1	The Hawthorns	3-4
08.12.1975	Mansfield Town	FA Cup Rd 2	Villa Park	1-2

whilst some of their FA Cup games against non-League opposition have been played on a neutral ground.

22.11.1952	Beighton MW	FA Cup Rd 1	Millmoor	3-0
21.11.1953	Horden Colliery	FA Cup Rd 1	Millmoor	1-0
27.02.1978	Blyth Spartans	FA Cup Rd 5	St James' Park	2-1
20.11.1982	Holbeach Utd	FA Cup Rd 1	London Road	4-0

The club's Welsh Cup semi-finals were of course played on neutral grounds as were many of their appearances in the Welsh Cup Final.

NICKNAMES

Wrexham's nickname is the Robins named after Ted Robinson who played in 297 first team games between 1894 and 1907 and not because of the club's red and white strip. Robinson himself was nick-named 'Mac' because he often wore a mackintosh. Also many other players in the club's history have been fondly known by their nicknames. They include:

Billy Ashcroft	(1970-1977)	'King Billy'
Jon Bowden	(1987-1992)	'Animal'
Bill Davies	(1902-1905)	'Tinker'
Brian Tinnion	(1969-1976)	'Budgie'

NIEDZWIECKI, EDDIE

Born in Bangor, goalkeeper Eddie Niedzwiecki was the son of a Pole who came to Britain during the Second World War. A former Welsh Schoolboy and Youth international, he made his debut for Wrexham in a 2-2 home draw against Oxford United in August 1977, but then only played in 27 League games over the next four seasons, as he deputised for the more experienced Brian Lloyd and Dai Davies.

When the latter returned to the Vetch Field to play for Swansea at the end of the 1980-81 season, Niedzwiecki replaced him between the posts and was ever-present the following season when he kept 12 clean sheets despite Wrexham being relegated from the Second Division. In 1982-83 he missed just four games as the Robins suffered another relegation into the League's basement.

However, Niedzwiecki's performances led to Chelsea paying £45,000 for his services and in five seasons at Stamford Bridge, he made 136 League appearances and won a Second Division championship medal. Capped twice by Wales at full international level, he sadly had to quit the game at the age of 29 after five operations on his knee. He stayed at Stamford Bridge as youth team coach before becoming assistant-manager and later reserve team coach.

NOCK, JACK

Jack Nock played his first League football with Leicester Fosse and Merthyr Tydfil before leaving to play non-League football with Cradley Heath. In 1922 he returned to League football with Cardiff City and though he was on the fringe of the first team for several seasons, he only made two League appearances before in November 1924, joining Wrexham.

He played his first game for the club in a 1-1 draw at home to Walsll and though he failed to get on the score sheet, it wasn't long before he rediscovered his scoring touch as he netted a hat-trick in a 6-2 home win over Wigan Borough. He ended the season with 10 goals in 25 League appearances and won a Welsh Cup winners' medal as Flint Town were defeated 3-1.

In 1925-26 he scored 12 goals in 40 League games but at the end of the season he was allowed to leave the Racecourse Ground and after a spell out of the game, he again teamed up with former Wrexham manager Charlie Hewitt at Flint Town.

NON-LEAGUE

'Non-League' is the shorthand term for clubs which are not members of the Football League. Since Wrexham entered the Football League in 1921-22, they have met non-League opposition in the FA Cup on a number of occasions. The club's record is:

Date	Opposition	FA Cup Stage	Venue	Score
19.11.1921	Burton All Stars	Qualifying 4th	Home	4-0
02.12.1926	Rhyl	Round 2	Away	1-3
14.12.1929	Manchester Central	Round 2	Away	1-0
13.12.1930	Wellington Town	Round 2	Away	4-2
26.11.1932	Spennymoor United	Round 1	Home	3-0
28.11.1936	Blyth Spartans	Round 1	Away	2-0
30.11.1946	Marine	Round 1	Home	5-0
26.11.1949	Grantham	Round 1	Home	4-1
22.11.1952	Beighton M.W.	Round 1	Away*	3-0
06.12.1952	Yarmouth Town	Round 2	Away	2-1
21.11.1953	Horden Colliery	Round 1	Away*	1-0
20.11.1954	Netherfield	Round 1	Away	3-3
24.11.1954	Netherfield	Round 1(R)	Home	3-1
14.11.1959	Blyth Spartans	Round 1	Home	2-1
05.11.1960	Bangor City	Round 1	Away	0-1
20.11.1963	Altrincham	Round 1	Away	0-0
27.11.1963	Altrincham	Round 1(R)	Home	3-0
14.11.1964	Macclesfield Town	Round 1	Away	2-1
13.11.1965	South Liverpool	Round 1	Home	4-1
15.11.1969	Spennymoor United	Round 1	Away	4-1
11.12.1971	Wigan Athletic	Round 2	Home	4-0
20.11.1976	Gateshead	Round 1	Home	6-0
11.12.1976	Goole Town	Round 2	Home	1-1
14.12.1976	Goole Town	Round 2(R)	Away	1-0
26.11.1977	Burton Albion	Round 1	Home	2-0
18.02.1977	Blyth Spartans	Round 5	Home	1-1
27.02.1977	Blyth Spartans	Round 5(R)	Away**	2-1
20.11.1982	Holbeach United	Round 1	Away***	4-0
11.12.1982	Worcester City	Round 2	Away	1-2
19.11.1988	Runcorn	Round 1	Away	2-2
22.11.1988	Runcorn	Round 1(R)	Home	2-3
16.11.1991	Winsford United	Round 1	Home	5-2
07.12.1991	Telford United	Round 2	Home	1-0
16.11.1996	Colwyn Bay	Round 1	Away	1-1
26.11.1996	Colwyn Bay	Round 1(R)	Home	2-0

* Played at Millmoor; ** Played at St James' Park; *** Played at London Road

NORTHERN SECTION CUP

In their first match in the inaugural competition in 1933-34, the Robins beat New Brighton 11-1 with Tommy Bamford scoring five of the goals and William Bryant a hat-trick to progress into the second round, where Bryant scored both goals in a 2-0 home win over Chester. The third round saw Wrexham travel to Crewe Alexandra and though the home side provided stubborn opposition, goals from Bamford and Bulling gave the Robins a 2-1 win and a place in the semi-final. Sadly, despite George Snow netting for Wrexham, their opponents Darlington proved to be the stronger side on the day and won 3-1.

In 1934-35, Wrexham drew 1-1 at home to Chester before losing to the only goal of the game in the replay at Sealand Road. It was a similar story in 1935-36 when two goals from Archie Burgon enabled the Robins to draw 2-2 against the Cestrians at the Racecourse Ground but in the replay Wrexham were well beaten 4-0.

The Robins went out at the first hurdle in 1936-37, losing 1-0 at New Brighton and the Rakers also triumphed in the first round the following season, winning 2-0.

The club's last season in the competition, 1938-39, saw them beat Crewe Alexandra 2-1 before meeting New Brighton in round two. After being held 1-1 at home, the Robins travelled to Raikes Lane and in an entertaining match lost 4-3 after extra-time with Bert Nelson scoring two of Wrexham's goals.

OLDEST PLAYER

The oldest player to line-up in a Wrexham first team is William Lot Jones. He was 46 years old when he played his last game for the club against Tranmere Rovers (Home 1-3) in a Third Division (North) game on 22nd April 1922.

OWEN, GARETH

Midfield general Gareth Owen graduated through Wrexham's youth ranks before making his first team debut as a substitute in a 4-2 home win over Aldershot in September 1990.

He has represented Wales at both Under-21 and 'B' international level where he reproduced the surging runs which are a feature of his midfield play. There are many at the Racecourse Ground who felt that the Chester-born player would by now be playing at a higher level, but he has suffered with both injuries and inconsistent performances in recent seasons.

Possessing a powerful shot, Owen has now scored 29 goals in 321 first team games for Wrexham and whilst all Robins' fans would like to see him on the score sheet more often, many would settle for a return to the form of his first few seasons at the Racecourse Ground.

P

PARKER, ALBERT

After beginning his career with Everton as a schoolboy, he joined South Liverpool, only to find his career interrupted by the Second World War.

After the hostilities had ended, he joined Crewe Alexandra and in three seasons at Gresty Road made 111 appearances before signing for Wrexham in November 1951. He played his first game for the club in a 2-1 defeat at Darlington a few days after putting pen to paper and went on to give the club eight years loyal service.

Parker was a tough-tackling full-back and able to play on either flank and though he appeared in 248 first team games for the club, he only scored one goal. However, it was a most unusual goal and came in the 3-0 home defeat of Workington on 1st October 1952. He hit a 'shot' from fully 70 yards that bounced over the Workington 'keeper to open the scoring for the Robins.

He left the Racecourse Ground in 1959 but after a season of playing non-League football for Holywell Town, he returned to become Wrexham's grounds man. He later took up refereeing and once ran the line in an Inter Cities Fairs Cup match. In 1977 he returned to the Racecourse Ground for a third time as a gate man.

PENALTIES

On 13th December 1947, Wrexham travelled to play Colchester United who were then a non-League club, in the second round of the FA Cup. The Robins were losing 1-0 with just a few minutes remaining when they were awarded a penalty. Billy Tunnicliffe, the club's regular penalty taker ran up to take the kick and promptly fainted! Centre-forward Jack Boothway then ran up to take the spot-kick but as he shot, he stubbed his toe and the ball trickled gently into the arms of the Colchester 'keeper – Wrexham were out of the FA Cup.

On 19th January 1980, Dixie McNeil was sent-off as he was waiting to take a penalty kick that had been awarded to Wrexham in the dying minutes of their Second Division League match against Charlton Athletic. Whilst McNeil was waiting to take the spot-kick a number of the Charlton players resorted to some gamesmanship tactics, resulting in the Wrexham forward losing his patience and kicking the ball into the crowd. He was immediately sent-off by the referee who had booked him earlier in the match. However, the game did have a happy ending for the Welsh club as Mick Vinter stepped up to score from the spot to give Wrexham a 3-2 win.

PHILLIPS, WAYNE

Wayne Phillips burst onto the first team scene with a stunning goal in a Welsh Cup tie against Rhyl on 6th February 1990, and four days later made his Football League debut in a goal-less draw at home to Hereford United.

Now having played in 239 first team games fort he Robins over the last eight seasons, he prefers a more central role in midfield, though he has also filled in at right-back and in central defence. A Welsh 'B' international, he likes to be involved and loves to test the opposition 'keeper from long range.

In 1995-96 his form was so impressive that Wales manager Bobby Gould included the Bangor-born player on the bench during the friendly against Switzerland at Lugano in April 1996. That season he was voted the club's Player of the Year and if he can avoid injuries there is no reason why he shouldn't win that full cap in the near future.

PHYTHIAN, ERNIE

A former England Youth international player, he began his career with his home-town club, Bolton Wanderers. But after three years as a professional in which he scored three goals in just 11 first team appearances, he joined Wrexham in March 1962, in the part-exchange deal that saw Wyn Davies sign for the Wanderers.

He made his debut in a 1-0 defeat at Darlington but went on to score three goals in the last 13 games of the season to help the Robins win promotion to the Third Division. In 1962-63 he scored his first hat-trick for the club in a 5-1 home win over Millwall and the following season was the club's leading scorer as they made a quick return to the League's basement. His 20 League goals included another hat-trick in the 4-0 defeat of Notts. County at the Racecourse Ground. He continued to be amongst the goals in 1964-65 but at the end of the season he left Wrexham to join Hartlepool United, having scored 48 goals in 161 first team games.

In three seasons at Hartlepool, he scored 50 goals in 124 League games before going to play in South Africa.

PITCH

The Racecourse Ground pitch measures 111 yards by 71 yards.

PLASTIC

There have been four Football League clubs that replaced their normal grass playing pitches with artificial surfaces at one stage or another. Queen's Park Rangers were the first in 1981 but the Loftus Road plastic was discarded in 1988 in favour of a return to turf. Luton Town, Oldham Athletic and Preston North End followed. Wrexham never played on the Kenilworth Road or Boundary Park plastic but drew 1-1 with Queen's Park Rangers on their only visit to the Loftus Road plastic on 16th January 1982, with Ian Edwards netting for the Robins. The club have played twice on the Deepdale plastic, but on each occasion have lost 1-0 to Preston North End.

PLAY-OFFS

After leading the Fourth Division table for most of the 1988-89 season, the Robins fell away and only by winning their last three games of the season did they qualify for the play-offs.

They met Scunthorpe United in the semi-final stage and after winning 3-1 at the Racecourse Ground with two goals from Ollie Kearns, did the double over their Lincolnshire opponents when two goals from Kevin Russell gave them a 2-0 victory and a place in the two-legged final. Their opponents were Leyton Orient and again the first leg was at the Racecourse Ground. Though the Robins had the better of the play, the game remained goal-less. The second leg at Brisbane Road was watched by 13,355 and was delayed by 20 minutes to allow the fans to get into the ground. The O's went into half-time 1-0 up but within minutes of the restart, Jon Bowden equalised. If the result had stayed at 1-1 then Wrexham would have been promoted on the away goals rule but just eight minutes from time, Mark Cooper scored the winner for Orient.

POINTS

Under the three points for a win system which was introduced in 1981-82, Wrexham's best points tally is the 80 points in 1992-93 when the club won promotion to Division Two. However, the club's best points haul under the old two points for a win system was the 61 points in seasons 1969-70 (when the club finished runners-up in the Fourth Division) and 1977-78 (when they won the Third Division championship).

Wrexham's worst record under either system is the meagre 32 points secured in season's 1925-26, 1949-50 and 1963-64, the only one of the three seasons in which the club were relegated.

PROMOTION

Wrexham have been promoted on four occasions. They were first promoted in 1961-62 when new manager Ken Barnes led the club to third place in the Fourth Division behind Millwall and Colchester United. The highlight of the Robins' first promotion-winning season was the 10-1 defeat of Hartlepool United in which Roy Ambler, Ken Barnes and Wyn Davies all scored hat-tricks.

They were promoted a second time in 1969-70 when they finished runners-up in the Fourth Division to Chesterfield.

In 1977-78 they were promoted for a third time when they won the Third Division championship, finishing three points ahead of Cambridge United. The club clinched promotion with a 7-1 home win over Rotherham United in which Graham Whittle netted a hat-trick to bring Second Division football to the Racecourse Ground for the first time.

Wrexham were last promoted in 1992-93 when they finished the season three points adrift of Third Division champions, Cardiff City.

Q

QUICKEST GOAL

Eddie Beynon holds the club record for scoring the fastest goal when he netted with a powerful 35-yard header in a 6-0 win in the Welsh Cup at Chester on 12th January 1949.

R

RACECOURSE GROUND

Apart from four seasons in which the club played at the Recreation Ground in Rhosddu, Wrexham have played at the Racecourse Ground since their formation in September 1872.

Up until the football club's formation, the Racecourse was used mainly for cricket, though horse racing had also been featured there until an exception was taken to the behaviour of race-goers.

In one corner of the pitch was the Turf Hotel and it was here that members of the cricket club formed a football club. Wrexham first played on the cricket pitch in the middle of the racecourse. This was also the venue for the first-ever Welsh home international in March 1877, when Scotland were the visitors.

At the end of the 1879-80 season, the club moved from the Racecourse Ground and played at the nearby Rhosddu Recreation Ground.

The Racecourse Ground as we know it today began to take shape in 1902 when the pitch was realigned from east to west in readiness for the Wales v England international match on 3rd March 1902. At that time the Racecourse Ground was described as being surrounded by a cycle track and having banking on three sides.

Following Wrexham's admission to the Football League in 1921, ground designer Archibald Leitch was asked to consider a redevelopment but the next development was in 1926 when a Supporters' Club was formed. The first £300 raised paid for the erection of a cover behind the Plas Coch goal, which is the end behind which the Technical College is now situated. Three years later, a further £500 was spent to extend the shelter behind the same goal, It was later extended around the side of the playing area at a cost of £2,000.

During the 1930s the Mold Road Stand was extended by a wing stand which became known as the Plas Coch Stand.

After the Second World War, new changing rooms were installed under the Mold Road and Plas Coch Stands and the Town End of the Racecourse Ground had concrete terracing laid down.

On 26th January 1957, the Racecourse Ground housed its largest

ever crowd when 34,445 turned up to see Manchester United win an FA Cup fourth round match 5-0..

Floodlights were added in 1959 at a cost of £14,000 and on 30th September, 15,555 witnessed the first floodlight game when Wrexham lost 2-1 to Swindon Town.

After the club had won promotion to the Third Division in 1961-62 the fans spent £4,000 on one of the oddest structures ever to grace a Football League ground. The frame and seats of the local Majestic Cinema that had recently closed down were placed on the Town End of the ground to provide a further 1,000 seats and also offer shelter, refreshment bar and club shop. Nicknamed the 'Pigeon Loft' it was eventually demolished in 1978 after it had been deemed unsafe.

In 1971, a decision was taken to modernise the Racecourse Ground in an attempt to restore Wrexham's status as a regular international venue. The following year, in time for the club's European debut, the first new stand was built on the Popular side with 2,750 seats and a paddock. Called the Yale Stand, this became the club's Main Stand. Later the underneath of the stand housed new dressing-rooms, club offices, entertainment suites and the Centenary Club for supporters.

In 1978 shortly after the club had won promotion to the Second Division, a similar Stand called the Border Stand, seating 2,250 was opened at the Plas Coch end. It was named the Border Stand after the local brewery which owned the ground.

In 1985, the Mold Road Stand and the Plas Coch Stand were deemed to be unsafe and had to be closed because of the newly-imposed safety measures.

In 1990 the Racecourse Ground had an electronic scoreboard fixed to the top of the Border Stand and a year later, plans were unveiled to transform Wrexham's ground into a 15,000 capacity all-seater stadium with two new stands on Mold Road and at the Town End. There were also plans for the £44 million development to include a new social club, bowling alley, theme pub, swimming pool, cinema, conference centre, night club, hotel restaurants and two multi-storey car parks. However, since then, the club have put in formal planning permission for a new 3,500 seater stand to go along the Mold Road side of the ground, which will then get the Racecourse back to a four-sided ground at last. The new stand will also house eight executive boxes.

Funding for the project is coming from the Football Trust, Sportslot, and the WDA and though they are still a number of legal snags to be overcome, the building of this much needed stand will bring the Racecourse Ground up to the standards required for the new millennium and increase the ground capacity to around 15,500.

RAPID SCORING

Though there have been a number of instances of rapid scoring in a Wrexham game, the Robins' 10-1 defeat of Hartlepool United on 3rd March 1962, was perhaps the most impressive.

Wyn Davies whose last game for the club this was, opened the scoring after six minutes and three minutes later, added a second. The future Welsh international who was to join Bolton Wanderers after this game, completed his hat-trick in the 24th minute. Ron Barnes added a fourth in the 28th minute before Hartlepool pulled a goal back and then he made it 5-1 on the stroke of half-time.

In the second half Wrexham scored five goals in the space of 15 minutes. Roy Ambler made it 6-1 in the 55th minute before Ron Barnes completed his hat-trick a minute later. Ambler scored his second in the 64th minute and then Stan Bennion made it 9-1 two minutes later. Ambler netted his third goal in the 70th minute to take Wrexham's score into double figures but despite there being 20 minutes still to play, the Robins failed to add to their score.

RECEIPTS

The club's record receipts are £126,012 for the FA Cup fourth round replay match against West Ham United on 4th February 1992. For the record, the Robins lost 1-0 after drawing 2-2 at Upton Park.

RE-ELECTION

Wrexham have had to apply for re-election to the Football League on just one occasion and that was in 1965-66 when they finished bottom of the Fourth Division. The Robins won only one of their last 13 matches, but thankfully were re-elected with ease.

REGAN, TED

Signed from Crichton's Athletic in the summer of 1921, primarily as cover for the club's wing-halves, he was called upon to make his debut at centre-forward in the match against Accrington Stanley on 29th October, after an injury to Bill Cotton. He scored both goals in Wrexham's 2-1 win and in the next match, scored the club's first hat-trick in the Football League as Chesterfield were beaten 6-1. Yet despite this start, it was the following season before he became a regular in the Wrexham side, reverting back to his customary wing-half position.

He won a Welsh Cup winners' medal in 1924 but was disappointed to miss the club's first competitive match against top flight opposition when they played Birmingham City in a fourth round FA Cup match. Regan went on to play in 216 first team games for the Robins before joining one of the top non-League sides of the time, Manchester Central.

RELEGATION

Wrexham have been relegated on only four occasions. Their first taste came in 1959-60 when manager John Love was relieved of his duties after the club had lost 11 of its first 19 games. Cliff Lloyd once again took temporary charge of the team but sadly he failed to turn things round and the Robins conceded 101 goals in finishing 23rd in the

Third Division to be relegated to the Fourth Division for the first time in their history.

Wrexham were next relegated in 1963-64 after regaining their Third Division status the previous season. The Robins conceded 107 goals in this campaign and failed to win until their sixth match of the season when they beat Colchester United 5-4. After they had demolished Barnsley 7-2 at the Racecourse Ground at the end of September, they lost their next nine matches including a 9-0 thrashing at Brentford, which remains the club's record defeat. Again the Welsh side finished 23rd in the Third Division and returned to the League's basement.

The club's third experience of relegation came in 1981-82 when once again they began the season without a win until their sixth match. The rest of the campaign continued to be dismal and at the end of the season, Wrexham were in 21st position and were relegated to the Third Division.

The club's last experience of relegation came the following season, 1982-83, when they suffered the drop in successive seasons, this time to the Fourth Division.

RHOSDDU RECREATION GROUND

At the end of the 1879-80 season, Wrexham were forced to leave the Racecourse Ground after the cricket club, who then owned the ground, increased the rent. They moved to play their matches at the Recreation Ground in Rhosddu. The admission prices at the Recreation Ground for the 1880-81 season was three pence (2p) 'in the ground' whilst to watch the game from the enclosure or the grandstand cost sixpence (3p). Wrexham were to play at the Rhosddu Recreation Ground for three seasons with one of the most prestigious matches being the visit of Everton for a friendly match on 11th November 1882, which Wrexham won 5-3.

RICHARDS, GORDON

Gordon Richards was playing for Ruabon when he was recommended to Cliff Lloyd. After winning Welsh Youth international honours he made his Wrexham debut in a 2-0 win at Mansfield Town in September 1952. A tricky outside-left, he won a regular place in the Robins' side the following season when he came into his own during the club's FA Cup match against Brighton and Hove Albion. He scored in the replay at the Goldstone Ground but the Seagulls netted a late equaliser to earn a second replay at Selhurst Park. In this match, the Robins triumphed 3-1 and Richards who scored with a diving header was knocked unconscious in the process.

An operation to remove a perforated appendix caused him to miss most of the 1954-55 season whilst bruised ribs restricted his appearances in 1956-57. He had scored 28 goals in 106 games for Wrexham when in January 1958, he was allowed to join Chester. He spent three years at Sealand Road, playing in 75 league games before a knee injury forced his retirement from League football.

ROBERTS, BOBBY

Bobby Roberts began his career with Motherwell, where he won Scottish Under-21 and Scottish League honours before coming south of the border to join Leicester City for £40,000 in September 1963. Initially he struggled at Filbert Street but was often played out of position. He missed the 1964 League Cup Final, despite scoring in both legs of the semi-final. The midfield anchorman gained an FA Cup runners-up medal in 1969 and went on to play in 281 games for Leicester, scoring 36 goals before moving to Mansfield Town. He played in 76 league games for the Field Mill club before coaching Coventry City.

His first managerial post was at Colchester United. They were relegated to the Fourth Division in 1976 but bounced straight back in third place the following season. In 1979 they reached the fifth round of the FA Cup before losing narrowly to Manchester United. The Layer Road club were relegated again in 1981 and when he failed to take them straight back up, he was sacked.

He became manager of Wrexham in the summer of 1982 but his first season in charge saw the club relegated for a second successive season, this time to the Fourth Division. The following season, 1983-84, the Robins just avoided having to apply for re-election after they beat Tranmere Rovers 5-1 in the last match of the season. This season saw Roberts come out of retirement when he played in goal in a 1-1 draw against Worcester City in the Welsh Cup!

He left the Racecourse Ground in March 1985, and after a year managing Grimsby Town, returned to Filbert Street as coach.

ROBERTS, JOHN

John Roberts started his professional career with his home-town club, Swansea Town in July 1964, and spent three years at Vetch Field before joining Northampton Town in November 1967. At the County Ground he made 62 League appearances before Arsenal paid £30,000 for his services in May 1969.

During his first full season at Highbury, he played in 11 League games, followed in 1970-71 by winning a League Championship medal, playing in 18 League games during Arsenal's Double season.

John Roberts

Also that season he won the first of his 22 Welsh caps when he played against England. In October 1972, after having played in 81 League and Cup games for the Gunners he joined Birmingham City for a fee of £140,000.

At St Andrew's, Roberts was constantly plagued by injuries and in four years with the club only appeared in 79 games.

In August 1976, Roberts joined Wrexham for £30,000 and made his debut in a 2-0 home win over Portsmouth on the opening day of the 1976-77 season. After the Robins finished fifth in his first season at the Racecourse Ground, Roberts inspired the club to the Third Division championship in 1977-78, scoring four goals in 41 appearances. Also that season he won a Welsh Cup winners' medal as Bangor City were beaten 3-1 on aggregate. He went on to play in 191 first team games for Wrexham before moving to Hull City for £15,000 in the summer of 1980.

He spent two seasons at Boothferry Park before having to retire through injury.

ROBINSON, TED

The man after whom the club's nickname of the Robins is named, Ted Robinson joined Wrexham in the summer of 1893 to begin 50 years service with the Welsh club. After a year of playing reserve football, he made his first team debut in the 11-1 Welsh League victory over Caergwrle Wanderers in October 1894.

He captained Wrexham to three successive Combination League championships from 1900-01 to 1902-03, missing just two games in the process. He also picked up three Welsh Cup winners' medals in 1897, 1903 and 1905 as well as five runners-up medals.

The tough-tackling centre-half played in 297 first team games for Wrexham before being appointed club secretary at the end of the 1905-06 season. He did turn out once more for the club, on 19th January 1907, when they were short. The Yorkshire-born Robinson gave a sound display in a 1-0 defeat at Molineux against Wolverhampton Wanderers Reserves.

He retired as secretary in 1929 when Jack Baynes was appointed as the club's manager but due to the Rexham boss' ill-health, he soon returned as financial secretary, a position he held until 1943. He also acted as the club's caretaker-manager for two matches, both of which were won!

ROGERS, BILLIE

After playing his early football with Oak Alyn and Flint, mainly at wing-half or inside-forward, he joined Wrexham in the summer of 1926. He scored a goal on his debut in a 3-1 home win over Chesterfield on the opening day of the 1926-27 season and ended the campaign with nine goals in 33 League games. Also during the course of that season, he scored all four goals in the club's 4-1 win at Llandudno in the fifth round of the Welsh Cup.

Over the next six seasons, he proved himself to be one of the club's most versatile players, wearing seven different numbered outfield shirts.

At the end of the 1928-29 season in which he was an ever-present, he toured Canada with Wales before making his full international debut against Scotland in 1931. He won another cap when England visited the Racecourse Ground but in the summer of 1932 after scoring 29 goals in exactly 200 first team games, he joined Newport County.

His stay at Somerton Park was short and after a spell with Bristol Rovers, he ended his League career with Clapton Orient. Later he played non-League football for Bangor City, but sadly just a year after hanging up his boots, he became ill and died, aged just 31.

ROWLEY, JACK

One of the most prolific goal-scorers in the history of Manchester United, Jack Rowley began his career with his home-town club Wolverhampton Wanderers but failed to make the first team. Third Division Bournemouth spotted his potential and signed him up in 1936. Within a couple of months he had made his League debut and before the year was out, had been transferred to United for £3,000. After a bright start, he faded and spent six weeks in the reserves before returning to first team action at centre-forward to knock in four goals as United thrashed Swansea 5-1. Rowley was to hang on to the number nine shirt for the next 18 years!

Though the war interrupted his Old Trafford career, he 'guested' for a number of clubs including Wolves and Spurs, scoring eight in one game for the Molineux club and seven in another for Spurs. During the wartime season of 1941-42 he scored 34 goals in 15 games including seven against New Brighton. When League football resumed in 1946-47, Rowley had matured into a strong, bustling centre-forward and scored 28 goals. He played six times for England, winning his first cap against Switzerland in 1948. He also played for the England 'B' side, the Football League and in a wartime international.

With United he won an FA Cup winners' medal in 1948, scoring twice as the Reds beat Blackpool 4-2 and then hit a record breaking 30 League goals as United clinched the championship in 1952.

In all he scored 208 goals for United in 422 games, the third highest scorer in the club's history.

Given a free transfer in 1955 he became player-manager of Plymouth Argyle. He took some time to rebuild the Home Park club, but the board's patience was rewarded in 1959 when Argyle returned to the Second Division. He left the club suddenly but was soon back in football as manager of Oldham Athletic. He brought about a steady improvement each season and in 1962-63, the Latics won promotion. Three days later, a dispute arose between Rowley and the board and he left as the club were still celebrating their success.

After working abroad with Ajax of Amsterdam he returned in January 1966, to become manager of Wrexham. Sadly, he could do nothing to stop the rot that had already set in and at the end of the 1965-66 season, the club had to seek re-election for the only time in their history. The following season there was a marked improvement and the Robins finished seventh.

He left the Racecourse Ground in April 1967, to manage Bradford Park Avenue, later returning to manage Oldham Athletic for a second spell. After relegation and more poor results, he was sacked.

RUSH, IAN

A Schoolboy international from the tiny Welsh village of St Asaph, he started his career with Chester. After just 34 League appearances, which had yielded 14 goals, Liverpool manager Bob Paisley paid £30,000 for the youngster. He became a full international over six months before his first team debut as Liverpool took care not to rush him. His first goal for Wales came in May 1982 against the Irish at the Racecourse Ground. By this time, he had been blooded at Anfield and become a firm favourite of the Kop.

In 1981-82 he scored 30 goals in 49 games to win his first League Championship medal. There were further League titles in 1983 and 1984, European Cup victory in 1984 and League Cup wins in 1983 and 1984. The derby game with Everton in 1982-83 saw Liverpool rout the Blues at Goodison 5-0 with Rush netting four. In 1983-84 Ian Rush won the Golden Boot Award with his 32 goals scored in Division One matches. Perhaps the peak of his career was 1986 when the Anfield side lifted the near-impossible League and Cup double with Rush scoring twice in the 3-1 FA Cup Final victory over Everton.

Rush's reputation as one of the world's most feared strikers had clubs battling for his signature. Juventus succeeded in a deal worth

£3.2 million. There was one consolation for Liverpool fans in that he would be staying for one more season. He showed his greatness by playing his heart out and scoring 30 goals in 42 League games. When Rush left for Italy in 1987 he had overtaken Kenny Dalglish's club record of 116 League goals and reached a total of 207 in all competitions.

Following an unhappy time in Italy, Rush returned to Anfield in a sensational £2.8 million transfer just before the start of the 1988-89 season. Coming on as substitute in the 1989 FA Cup Final against Everton, Rush scored two goals as Liverpool won 3-2 after extra-time, taking his total of derby goals to 21 to pass Dixi Dean's record of long ago. Capped 73 times by Wales, he left Anfield in May 1996 after scoring 346 goals in 659 first team games including 229 League goals, second only to Roger Hunt's 245.

Joining Leeds United on a free transfer, he hit the worst goal-scoring drought of his long career and left Elland Road to play for Newcastle United. His first goal for the Magpies came in the Coca Cola Cup against Hull City, taking his career total to 49 and equalling Geoff Hurst's competition record. He also hit a third round FA Cup winner against Everton, extending his record as the top FA Cup goal-scorer this century. After being released in the summer of 1998, Rush signed for Wrexham as player-coach and made his first team debut in a 3-0 home win over Reading on the opening day of the 1998-99 season. He showed some brilliant touches to keep the line moving and is obviously a great catch by Wrexham manager Brian Flynn.

RUSSELL, KEVIN

An England Youth international, Kevin 'Rooster' Russell served his apprenticeship at Brighton and Hove Albion before joining Portsmouth in 1984. He played only occasionally at first team level at Fratton Park and in the summer of 1987 he was transferred to Wrexham, where he enjoyed by far the most productive years of his League career.

After making his debut in a disastrous 6-1 defeat at Torquay United on the opening day of the 1987-88 season he went on to top the club's scoring charts with 25 League and Cup goals including a hat-trick in a 3-0 home win over Exeter City. Twenty-seven goals followed in 1988-89 including a hat-trick in a 4-2 home win over Burnley. His goals drove the Robins into the Fourth Division play-offs where they lost in the two legged final to Leyton Orient.

Within weeks, Russell who had scored 52 goals in 108 matches for Wrexham was on his way to Leicester City for £100,000 but in three years at Filbert Street he was unable to command a regular first team place. Then after loan spells at Peterborough, Cardiff, Hereford and Stoke, he was recalled by the Filberts to score five goals during their run-in to the Second Division play-offs in 1992.

That summer he joined Stoke City permanently for £95,000 and played his part as the Potters won the new Second Division championship. At the end of that season he joined Burnley for £150,000 but after just six goals in 40 games he was on the move again, this time to Bournemouth. A year later he moved to Notts. County before in the summer of 1995 returning to the Racecourse Ground.

Until midway through the 1997-98 campaign, Russell hardly missed a game in his second spell with the Robins. He continued to score some important goals and in Wrexham's third round FA Cup replay at West Ham United in January 1997, he scored the only goal of the game in the 90th minute and followed it with two in the next round as the Robins won 4-2 at Peterborough United.

Now employed in an attacking midfield role, he combines a fine work rate and industry with the ability to be able to add to his impressive strike-rate.

S

SALATHIEL, NEIL

Wrexham-born Neil Salthiel was offered an apprenticeship by Sheffield Wednesday but was not keen to leave the area and approached the Robins. The Hillsborough club agreed to him signing for Wrexham and on 25th October 1980, at the age of 17 years 340 days, he made his debut in a 1-0 win at Queen's Park Rangers. He had made three more appearances when Arfon Griffiths was forced to sell him to Crewe Alexandra but a few weeks later, the Gresty Road club manager Tony Waddington was sacked and replaced by Arfon Griffiths!

Neil Salathiel

Salathiel went on to make 65 League appearances for the Railwaymen before playing for South African side Arcadia Shepherds.

In December 1983, he returned to the Racecourse Ground on a non-contract basis before signing a full contract in February 1984. In his second spell with the Robins he won a Welsh Cup winners' medal in 1986 and played in three European campaigns, but after 325 first team games, he was surprisingly allowed to leave the club at the end of the 1989-90 season.

He then had short spells with Telford United and Northwich Victoria before joining Newtown.

SALMON, MIKE

Mike Salmon

After making just one Football League appearance for Blackburn Rovers, the Leyland-born goalkeeper went on loan to Chester, where he appeared in 18 League and Cup games before being given a free transfer by Rovers at the end of the 1982-83 season.

Salmon joined Stockport County and after making his debut against York City on the opening day of the 1983-84 season, played in 134 consecutive games. In the summer of 1986 he joined Bolton Wanderers who were then in the Third Division, but after 36 first team appearances he joined Wrexham on loan.

His first game for the Robins was in a 1-0 defeat

at Cambridge United but after that, he kept seven clean sheets in 17 League appearances. At the end of the season he returned to Bolton but during the summer, Dixie McNeil splashed out £20,000 for him. Over the next two seasons, Salmon was a virtual ever-present and in 1988-89 helped the club to the play-offs but after playing in 117 games he left the Racecourse Ground to join First Division Charlton Athletic for £100,000. Now in his ninth season with the Addicks, he has played in almost 200 games.

SECOND DIVISION

Wrexham have had two spells in the Second Division. After winning the Third Division championship in 1977-78, the Robins entertained Brighton and Hove Albion for their first-ever game in Division Two. A crowd of 14,081 saw both sides fail to score, though Dixie McNeil went close on a number of occasions. The Robins then won their next two games, both away, 1-0 at Fulham and by the same score line at Orient and goalkeeper Dai Davies didn't concede a goal until the club's fifth game. Sadly, Wrexham didn't maintain this form and had to settle for 15th place. The next two seasons saw the club finish 16th on both occasions before in 1981-82 the Robins first spell in the Second Division ended when they were relegated. It was a disastrous season which the club began without a victory until their sixth match, although they did string together a run of eight unbeaten matches in mid-season.

The club's second spell in Division Two began in 1993-94 following reorganisation by the Football League. In that first season back in the Second Division, the Robins finished 12th with Gary Bennett scoring 32 of the club's 66 League goals to finish second to Reading's Jimmy Quinn in the divisional goal-scoring charts. It was a similar story the following season, the Robins finishing 13th and Bennett netting 29 of the club's 65 League goals but this time he headed the national scoring charts. In 1995-96 the club came close to reaching the play-offs but had to settle for eighth place, an improvement of five places from the previous campaign. The Robins repeated the achievement the following season, only this time they secured 69 points, one less than in 1995-96. Last season, 1997-98, the club looked certain to be involved in the play-offs but towards the end of the campaign results went against them and they ended the season in seventh place losing out to Fulham on goal difference.

SERTORI, MARK

Despite playing for Manchester Boys, he had left school when Stockport County offered him his chance in League football. Unable to make much of an impression at Edgeley Park, he followed his former County boss Colin Murphy to Lincoln City. After helping the Imps regain their Football League status, he lost his place in the Sincil Bank club's first team and joined Wrexham in February 1990, for a fee of £30,000.

He made his League debut for the Robins in a goal-less draw at home to Hereford United before going on to play in 18 games and help them avoid the drop to the Conference. Brian Flynn then switched him to a central defensive role and he went on to play in 135 first team games before following a loan spell at Witton Albion, he joined Bury on a free transfer at the end of the 1993-94 season.

In spite of being able to play in defence or attack, he found his opportunities at Gigg Lane limited and in July 1996, he moved to Scunthorpe United where he has proved to be a solid and reliable central defender.

Mark Sertori

SHERPA VAN TROPHY

The competition for Associate Members of the Football League was first sponsored for the 1987-88 season by Sherpa Van.

Wrexham's first match in the Sherpa Van Trophy saw them travel to Ninian Park where they lost 3-2 to Cardiff City and though Shaun Cunnington who scored in that game, netted in the second preliminary round game at home to Walsall, it finished 2-2 and so the Robins failed to reach the knockout stages of the competition.

In 1988-89, Wrexham drew 1-1 with Sheffield United at the Racecourse Ground before goals from Preece and Bowden gave them a 2-1 victory at Chester. This qualified the Robins for the knockout stages, where in the first round they drew Sheffield United, the Blades having qualified with Wrexham from their group. This time Wrexham triumphed 2-1 to set up a Northern Area quarterfinal tie with Bolton Wanderers at Burnden Park. The Robins were leading 1-0 and were easily the better team when the Wanderers got a late equaliser and went on to win 3-1 after extra-time.

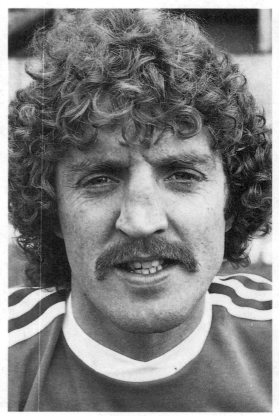

Bobby Shinton

SHINTON, BOBBY

Bobby Shinton began his League career with Walsall after joining the Saddlers from West Midlands club Lye Town. He scored 20 goals in 79 League appearances for Walsall before signing for Cambridge United in March 1974. After two seasons at the Abbey Stadium in which the

West Bromwich-born forward continued to find the net, 25 goals in 99 League games, he joined Wrexham for £15,000 in the summer of 1976.

He scored both Wrexham goals on his debut as Portsmouth were beaten 2-1 at the Racecourse Ground on the opening day of the 1976-77 season. That campaign saw him score 22 goals including a hat-trick in a 6-0 first round FA Cup win over Gateshead. In 1977-78 he was again on top form throughout a campaign which saw Wrexham win the Third Division championship and the Welsh Cup. At the end of the following season he left the Racecourse Ground after scoring 56 goals in 175 games to join Manchester City for £300,000.

His stay at Maine Road was brief and after only five League appearances and a loan spell at Millwall, he signed for Newcastle United for £175,000. In two years at St James Park, Shinton netted 10 goals in 42 games before moving to Millwall, where he ended his League career. He later had a short spell as player-manager of non-League Worcester City.

SHOWELL, GEORGE

George Showell began his Football League career with Wolverhampton Wanderers, but spent most of his early days at Molineux playing in the club's Central League side. After making his first team debut in a 1-1 draw against Preston North End in 1954, he did his National Service. On his return, he soon established himself as a first team regular and went on to play in 200 League games for the Molineux club and won an FA Cup winners' medal in 1960 when Wolves beat Blackburn Rovers 3-0.

After a short spell with Bristol City, where he made just 11 appearances, he joined Wrexham and made his debut in a 1-0 defeat at Stockport County. Sadly after just two seasons at the Racecourse Ground in which he played in 54 games he was forced to quit the playing side with a serious knee injury. He was then taken on the coaching staff and later became trainer, caretaker-manager and physiotherapist in 24 years service to the Robins.

Unfortunately in 1990 he had to resign his post as he was said to be unqualified under the new rules laid down by the F.A.

SMALLMAN, DAVID

David Smallman burst on to the scene in 1972-73 when he scored 15 goals in 40 League and Cup appearances. Having scored against Oldham Athletic and Notts. County in successive games, he kept his place for the club's European Cup Winners' Cup second round first leg tie against Hajduk Split and scored in a 3-1 win for the Robins. The following month he netted a hat-trick in a 5-0 FA Cup first round replay win over Darlington.

The following season was Smallman's best as his goals helped Wrexham reach the sixth round of the FA Cup for the first time in their history. In 1974-75 he topped the club's goal-scoring charts with 20 League and Cup goals and scored his second hat-trick for the Robins in a 4-0 home win over Aldershot which transpired to be his last appearance in a Wrexham shirt.

David Smallman

Capped three times by Wales in his Wrexham career, the Connah's Quay-born forward joined Everton for £75,000 and though he scored three goals in the first four games of the 1975-76 season, his five years at Goodison were nothing short of a disaster. Smallman who had scored 51 goals in 125 first team games for the Robins, broke his leg twice and managed just seven goals in 25 games.

After emigrating to Australia where he played part-time football, he returned to the Racecourse Ground to play in the club's Reserve side before playing non-League football with Newtown and Colwyn Bay.

SMITH, RAY

Centre-forward Ray Smith began his Football League career with Southend United after playing his early football with Basildon Motors. He made his first team debut shortly after turning professional in December 1961, and for the next three seasons was the club's leading scorer. He had scored 55 goals in 150 League games for the Roots Hall club when in the summer of 1967, Wrexham and former Southend United manager Alvan Williams paid £10,000 for Smith's services. He had only been at the Racecourse Ground for a matter of weeks when Charlton Athletic made the Robins an offer of £20,000 for the Islington-Born forward. Smith turned the move down and over the next five seasons proved himself one of the game's most skilful target men.

He made his Wrexham debut in the opening game of the 1967-68 season, scoring the Robins' goal in a 1-1 draw at home to Luton Town. He ended the campaign as the club's top scorer with 18 League goals including all the club' goals in a 5-3 defeat at Exeter City. His third hat-trick for the club came in a 4-2 home win over Colchester United in the Robins' promotion-winning season of 1969-70 when he formed a formidable partnership with Albert Kinsey. Injuries hampered his next two seasons at the Racecourse Ground and in July 1972, after he had scored 70 goals in 209 League and Cup games, he joined Peterborough United before ending his career playing non-League football for Bangor City.

SNOW, GEORGE

George Snow began his career as an inside-forward with Leeds United but having failed to make the grade joined Rochdale on a free transfer at the end of the 1931-32 season. The following campaign saw him score 13 goals in 41 League games for the Spotland club but in the summer of 1933 he was transferred to Wrexham.

He made his debut for the Robins in a 3-0 defeat at Barnsley on the opening day of the 1933-34 season but as the campaign wore on, his partnership with centre-forward Tommy Bamford flourished, the pair of them netting 61 of Wrexham's total of 99 League goals of which Snow's share was 17 goals. Following Bamford's transfer to Manchester United midway through the 1934-35 season, Snow became the club's top scorer with 18 League goals. He later switched to left-half and went onto appear in 225 League and Cup games for the club. Snow continued to play for Wrexham during the early years of wartime football, appearing in 33 matches.

SPEED, LES

Les Speed signed amateur forms for Wrexham just before the outbreak of the Second World War but because of the hostilities he failed to make his debut for the Welsh club until the game resumed in 1946-47. He joined the RAF and because he was based at Salisbury, he 'guested' for a number of clubs down south, including Brentford, Chelsea, Crystal Palace, Plymouth Argyle and Portsmouth. Though he was offered terms by the Fratton Park club he returned to Wrexham and made his League debut in a 1-1 draw at Carlisle United on 10th May 1947.

One of the club' great utility players, Les Speed appeared in all the outfield positions for the club, though most of his 241 first team appearances were at right-back.

In 1955 he left the Racecourse Ground to become player-manager of Stafford Rangers before later playing for Holywell Town. By now he had become a full-time blacksmith but later combined this with duties as Wrexham's youth team trainer.

SPONSORS

The club's official sponsors are Wrexham Lager.

STEEL, JIM

Dumfries-Born Jim Steel began his League career with Oldham Athletic where he scored 24 goals in 108 games before loan spells at Wigan and Wrexham. During his stay at the Racecourse Ground he scored six goals in nine outings and though the club wanted to buy him, they were having financial difficulties and couldn't afford the £10,000 fee. Steel joined Port Vale and helped the Valiants win promotion to the Third Division but midway through the 1983-84 season, he left Vale Park after there had been a managerial change and joined the Robins.

Many supporters expected instant goals after his previous exploits but his only goal in 29 games that season was one in the 3-2 win in the Associate Members Cup against Peterborough United.

However, the following season, Steel began to find the net with great regularity and was the club's leading scorer with 14 League goals. He scored a similar total in 1985-86 but also netted seven goals in the club's successful Welsh Cup campaign. He headed the club's scoring charts again in 1986-87 with 17 League goals and netted his first hat-trick in a 4-3 home win over Peterborough United.

His performances for the Robins in Europe led to FC Porto trying to sign him, but when the deal failed to materialise, he went on loan to Spanish side Real Coruna. Steel who had scored 72 goals in 230 games for Wrexham later joined Tranmere Rovers.

At Prenton Park he helped the Birkenhead club win promotion from the Fourth to the Second Division and played at Wembley in the Freight Rover Trophy final and play-offs but at the end of the 1991-92 season, Steel, who had scored 47 goals in 226 games for Rovers, left the game to join the Merseyside police force.

SUBSTITUTES

The first ever Wrexham substitute was David Campbell who came on for Martyn King against Doncaster Rovers at Belle Vue on 4th September 1965. The club's first goal-scoring substitute was Peter Wall who netted in the return fixture with Doncaster Rovers at the Racecourse Ground on 19th February 1966, as the Robins won 4-3.

The greatest number of substitutes used in a single season by Wrexham under the single substitute rule was 33 in 1978-79 but from 1986-87 two substitutes were allowed and in 1990-91, 63 were used. For the past couple of seasons, three substitutes have been allowed and in 1996-97, 75 were used.

The greatest number of substitute appearances for Wrexham has been made by Steve Buxton who came on during 50 League games

The line-up for 1979-80

with another 13 in cup ties. It was in 1995-96 that Steve Watkin re-wrote the Wrexham records on the matter of substitutes with 13 League appearances in the substitute's shirt.

SUNDAY FOOTBALL

The first-ever Sunday matches in the Football League took place on 20th January 1974 during the three-day week imposed by the government during the trial of strength with the coal-miners.

Wrexham travelled to Walsall on that date and in front of a 9,035 crowd went down 3-0.

SUSTAINED SCORING

During the 1933-34 season, Wrexham were battling with Barnsley and Chesterfield for the one promotion place to Division Two but though they scored 102 goals, they fell away to finish in sixth place. Tommy Bamford scored 44 goals in 41 games to set a League scoring record for the Robins. He scored five goals in an 8-1 home win over Carlisle United, all four in a 4-1 defeat of Doncaster Rovers and hat-tricks against Mansfield Town (Home 5-0) Gateshead (Away 3-0) and Walsall (Home 4-2).

SUTTON, MEL

An amateur with Aston Villa, Mel Sutton was released in December 1967, and immediately signed by Cardiff City manager Jimmy Scoular. He soon established himself in the Bluebirds' side and over the next four seasons made 138 League appearances before surprisingly being allowed to join Wrexham for £15,000 in July 1972.

He played his first game for the Robins at Southend United on the opening day of the 1972-73 season, scoring the only goal of the game.

Mel Sutton

Sutton proved to be one of the game's great bargains and in nine seasons as a player, appeared in 469 games for the club. He was one of three ever-presents in 1977-78 when the Robins won the Third Division championship and played in every FA Cup game that season when they reached the sixth round stage.

During that season, Sutton became player-assistant manager to Arfon Griffiths and when Griffiths resigned his post in May 1981, he was appointed manager in his place. Sadly, the 1981-82 season was not a happy one as Wrexham finished 21st in the Second Division and were relegated.

Relieved of his duties, he joined Arfon Griffiths at Crewe Alexandra but after a short stay at Gresty Road, he left the game.

T

TAPSCOTT, JOHNNIE

The cousin of Derek Tapscott, who played for Arsenal, Cardiff City and Wales, he was spotted playing junior football in his home-town of Plymouth and signed by Brighton and Hove Albion. Unable to break into the Seagulls' first team, he joined Leeds United but after only two months at Elland Road, where again he failed to make a first team appearance, he joined Wrexham.

He made his debut in a 1-0 home win over Shrewsbury Town on 30th August 1950, playing at inside-forward. Midway through the season he was switched to wing-half and he went on to be a virtual ever-present in that position for the next five seasons. In 1952-53 he missed just one game as the Robins almost won promotion to the Second Division, scoring his only goal of that campaign in a 3-1 Boxing Day win over Accrington Stanley.

Sadly, injury ended his career at the age of 28 after the popular Devonian had played in 192 games.

TELEVISION

Wrexham's first appearance on BBC's 'Match of the Day' was on 15th March 1975, when they beat Plymouth Argyle 3-0 at Home Park in a Division Three game with goals from Griffiths, Davies and Whittle.

The 'Match of the Day' cameras were at the Racecourse Ground on 4th January 1992, when Wrexham faced Arsenal in the third round of the FA Cup. The Welsh side had finished the previous season 92nd and last in the Football League, avoiding relegation only because there was no demotion to the GM Vauxhall Conference, while the League increased its numbers. Arsenal had been crowned League champions.

With eight minutes to go, Arsenal led 1-0 with a goal by Alan Smith. Then David O'Leary was penalised and 37-year-old Mickey Thomas blasted the free-kick wide of David Seaman's right hand. Two minutes later, Wrexham were ahead when 20-year-old Steve Watkin beat Tony Adams to the ball and rolled it past the England goalkeeper.

Andy Thackeray

THACKERAY, ANDY

Andy Thackeray began his career with Manchester City and played for them in the FA Youth Cup Final of 1986 when they beat Manchester United 3-1 over two legs. Surprisingly he was allowed to leave Maine Road and join his home-town club Huddersfield Town. However, there was great competition for places at Leeds Road and after only two League appearances he joined Newport County in March 1987, for a fee of £5,000.

The Somerton Park club were relegated at the end of that 1986-87 campaign and the following season were relegated to the Conference. Thackeray who had appeared in 62 first team games for Newport then joined Wrexham for the same fee that had taken him to County.

He made his debut for Wrexham in a 2-0 win at Exeter City on the opening day of the 1988-89 season and over the next four seasons he made the right-back spot his own and was ever-present in 1991-92. At the end of that season after playing in 195 games, he left the Racecourse Ground to join Rochdale for £15,000.

Appointed captain of the Spotland club, he suffered with long term injuries but still managed to appear in 195 games for the Lancashire club before being released at the end of the 1996-97 season.

THIRD DIVISION

Wrexham have had four spells in the Third Division. They lost their first-ever match in this division, which was also their first in the Football League, 2-0 at home to Hartlepool United and ended their first campaign in 12th place. The Robins played in the Third Division (North) for 30 seasons until 1957-58 when the new Third and Fourth Divisions were formed. They finished 12th that season and so started the following campaign in the higher division. The club had two seasons in this division before relegation in 1959-60.

Following promotion in 1961-62, the club's second spell in the Third Division lasted just two seasons before they were again relegated to the League's basement.

The Robins were promoted again in 1969-70 and this time their third spell in Division Three lasted eight seasons before they won promotion to the Second Division for the first time in their history. After four seasons of Second Division football, Wrexham were relegated to the Third Division in 1981-82 but after finishing 21st they went straight down to the Fourth Division following two successive relegations.

THOMAS, MICKEY

A Welsh Youth international, Mickey Thomas signed professional forms for Wrexham in April 1972, some three months after he made his debut on New Year's Day in a 4-0 defeat at Bournemouth. Over the next seven seasons, Thomas went on to appear in 299 first tem games for the Robins, winning a Third Division championship medal in 1977-78 and three Welsh Cup winners' medals. He also won 11 of his 51 Welsh caps whilst at the Racecourse Ground, his first coming against West Germany in 1977.

In November 1978, Manchester United paid Wrexham £300,000 to take Thomas to Old Trafford. He played in 110 League and Cup games for United including the 1979 FA Cup Final defeat by Arsenal. In July 1981, he signed for Everton in a deal which took John Gidman to

Mickey Thomas

Old Trafford. Thomas could not settle at Goodison and after just 11 first team games he moved to Brighton and Hove Albion for £400,000. His wife found it difficult to settle so far from her North Wales home and so in August 1982, Thomas moved to Stoke City for £200,000. In his first season at the Victoria Ground he won the Player of the Year award but in 1984, the Potters were forced to sell Thomas to Chelsea for only £75,000. From Stamford Bridge, he moved to West Bromwich Albion, and Derby County (on loan) before moving to the United States for 18 months and Witchita. On the return, it was Shrewsbury Town before a remarkable free transfer to Leeds United who, under Howard Wilkinson were just starting on their big push to the First Division. After drifting into the Reserves, Stoke took him on loan before he returned permanently on a free transfer.

In August 1991, he returned to the Racecourse Ground for a second

Mickey Thomas and (left) Tony Adams

spell and continued to make news on and off the field. He scored a brilliant free-kick goal against Arsenal in a memorable FA Cup giant-killing win and also had problems with some counterfeit notes!

TILSTON, TOMMY

Inside-forward Tommy Tilston began his Football League career with his home-town club Chester and scored six goals in 22 League appearances for the Cestrians before moving to Tranmere Rovers in the summer of 1951. However, he spent less than a seáson at Prenton Park, scoring 15 goals in 25 League games before being signed by Wrexham in March 1952.

He made his debut for the Robins against Crewe Alexandra, scoring one of the goals in a 4-0 win at the Racecourse Ground.

In 1952-53 when Wrexham finished third in Division Three (North), Tilston scored 17 goals in 43 League games, just one behind leading scorer Tommy Bannan. He continued to find the net the following season and scored a hat-trick in a 4-0 home win over Grimsby Town but in February 1954, after scoring 32 goals in 89 games he was allowed to leave the Racecourse Ground.

Tilston joined Crystal Palace who were struggling in the lower reaches of the Third Division (South) and in 58 League appearances for the Selhurst Park club, scored 14 goals before leaving in the summer of 1955.

TINNION, BRIAN

England Youth international Brian Tinnion began his League career with his home-town club Workington and played in 98 League games for the Cumbrian side before arriving at the Racecourse Ground for a then club record fee of £14,000.

After making his debut in a 3-0 home defeat by Colchester United in January 1969, Tinnion missed just one game until the end of the season. During the first part of the club's 1969-70 promotion-winning season, he provided the crosses for Albert Kinsey and Ray Smith to get on the score sheet before netting three himself in the last seven games of the campaign.

He won Welsh Cup winners' medals in 1972 and 1975 as the Robins

Brian Tinnion

beat Cardiff City on both occasions. An ever-present in seasons 1972-73 and 1973-74, he played in 122 consecutive League games for the club and in the latter season was the club's leading scorer. His 13 League goals in that campaign included hat-tricks against Southport (Home 3-2) and Plymouth Argyle (Home 5-2).

Tinnion had scored 65 goals in 335 games for the Robins when he left the Racecourse Ground in the summer of 1976 to play alongside Pele for New York Cosmos in the NASL.

TRANSFERS

Wrexham's current record transfer fee paid is £210,000, a figure they spent on buying back Joey Jones from Liverpool in October 1978. The club's record fee received is the £800,000 they got for Bryan Hughes when he joined Birmingham City in March 1997.

TUNNEY, EDDIE

Born on the Wirral, full-back Eddie Tunney began his career with Everton but after two years with the Goodison Park club in which he failed to make a first team appearance he left to join Wrexham.

He made his debut in a 2-1 home win over Bradford City in November 1937. A strong-tackling defender and a good distributor of the ball, he was an ever-present the following season and though the Second World War then interrupted his career, he was one of three Wrexham players to return to the club when the hostilities were over.

He was ever-present again in 1947-48 as the club finished third in Division Three (North), their highest League position since 1932-33 when they were runners-up. In 1949-50 he played in all five matches in the club's Welsh Cup exploits, though they lost 4-1 to Swansea Town in the final at Ninian Park.

Tunney played in 250 League and Cup games for Wrexham but after losing his place to Ray Williams, decided to retire.

TUNNICLIFFE, BILLY

Left-winger Billy Tunnicliffe began his League career with Port Vale, making his debut in a 2-1 home win against Rotherham United on 6th February 1937, but was unable to gain a regular place in the team and in May 1938, was given a free transfer. He then joined Bournemouth but returned to 'guest' for Vale during the war years. After the hostilities had ended he returned to Dean Court and in 10 appearances in the 1946-47 season scored one goal before signing for Wrexham.

He made his debut in a 1-0 win at Halifax Town on the opening day of the season and was the only ever-present in a Wrexham side that finished third in Division Three (North). In fact, not only was he Wrexham's top scorer with 21 League goals but he was also the highest-scoring winger in the Football League. He was ever-present again in 1948-49 and went on to play in 115 consecutive League games from his debut. A great favourite with the Wrexham crowd, he went on to score 90 goals in 264 League and Cup games in six seasons at the Racecourse Ground before leaving to join Bradford City.

He later played non-League football for Stafford Rangers and Congleton Town.

TWINS

David Jackson and his brother Peter are the only set of twins to have played League football for Wrexham. Peter Jackson is ten seconds older than his twin brother David. The Jacksons' career practically ran parallel with each other and their appearances for three League and three non-League clubs is unique. Peter Jackson made his League debut alongside his brother, playing for Wrexham in a 1-1 draw at home to Carlisle United on 2nd October 1954. When their father, who was the Wrexham manager left to join Bradford City, they saw the season out with Marine before joining Jackson senior at Valley Parade. When their father left City, the twins joined Tranmere Rovers. David left to play for Halifax and in the 1965 close season, Peter left Prenton Park to team up with David who had moved to Frickley Colliery. They later played together at Altrincham and Hyde United with Peter having spells at Macclesfield and Guiseley.

U

UNDEFEATED

Wrexham have remained undefeated at home throughout two League seasons: 1966-67 and 1969-70. The club's best and longest undefeated sequence at the Racecourse Ground in the Football League is of 38 matches between 25th January 1969, and 26th September 1970. Wrexham's longest run of undefeated Football League matches home and away is 16 between 3rd September 1966, and 2nd December 1966.

UNUSUAL GOALS

One of the most unusual goals in the history of Wrexham Football Club came from the boot of tough-tackling full-back Albert Parker on 1st October 1952, in the 3-0 home win over Workington. It was the Liverpool-born defender's only goal for the club in 248 first team appearances. He was fully 70 yards from goal when his 'shot' bounced over the Workington 'keeper!

UTILITY PLAYERS

A utility player is one of those particularly gifted footballers who can play in several or even many different positions. One of the club's earliest utility players in the Football League was Billie Rogers who

played in virtually every position except from goal although he pre-
ferred right-half or inside-forward.

Les Speed who played in 241 first team games between 1947 and
1955 played in all the outfield positions for the club.

After the mid 1960s, players were encouraged to become more
adaptable and to see their role as less stereotyped. At the same time
however, much less attention came to be paid to the implication of
wearing a certain numbered shirt and accordingly some of the more
versatile players came to wear almost all the different numbered
shirts at some stage or another, although this did not necessarily indi-
cate a vast variety of positions. In recent years both Mickey Evans and
Alan Hill have been talented enough to wear all the different numbered outfield shirts and both capable enough to deputise for an injured goalkeeper!

V

VICTORIES IN A SEASON – HIGHEST

In the 1969-70 season, Wrexham won 26 of their 46 League fixtures to
finish runners-up to Chesterfield in the Fourth Division, the highest
in the club's history.

VICTORIES IN A SEASON – LOWEST

Wrexham's poorest performance was in seasons 1923-24 and 1990-
91 when they won only ten of their League fixtures. In 1923-24 they
played 38 matches but in 1990-91 they played 46 matches and finished bottom of the Fourth Division.

VINTER, MICK

Mick Vinter began his footballing career with his home-town club
Boston United before joining Notts. County in March 1972. He went
on to score 53 goals in 148 League games for the Meadow Lane club
before asking for a transfer in the summer of 1979 after he thought his
game was getting stale.

Wrexham manager Arfon Griffiths paid £150,000 for Vinter's services and he made his debut in the club's first-ever Second Division game, scoring the only goal against West Ham United. He went on to score 17 goals in 45 League and Cup games including a hat-trick in a 6-0 FA Cup third round win over Charlton Athletic and both goals in the 5-2 fifth round defeat at Everton.

He continued to score for the club on a regular basis over the next two seasons but in 1981-82 his last season with the club, the Robins were relegated to the Third Division. In his last League match he scored a hat-trick in a 3-2 home win over Rotherham United and overall netted 42 goals in 131 first team games.

Vinter joined Oxford United and in two years at the Manor Ground he scored 21 goals in 69 League games before moving to Mansfield Town. He ended his League career with Newport County before playing non-League football for Gainsborough Tinity, Sutton Town, Matlock Town as well as having a short spell with his first club, Boston United.

VOUCHERS

When Wrexham were about to meet Manchester United in an FA Cup tie, a crowd of 18,069 turned up for a reserve match against Winsford United in the Cheshire League because vouchers were available for the cup game. The majority of the crowd left as soon as they acquired their Cup voucher and quite a number queued up again to get another voucher for a friend or relative.

WALES

Wrexham have provided more international players for Wales than any other club in the British Isles has supplied for one of the four home international teams. By the end of the 1997-98 season, there had been a total of 78 who had worn the colours of Wales while on the books of the oldest club in the Principality.

Steve Watkin

WARTIME FOOTBALL

In spite of the outbreak of war in 1914, the football leagues embarked upon their planned programme of matches for the ensuing season and these were completed on schedule at the end of April the following year. The season saw Wrexham finish sixth in the Birmingham and District League and win the Welsh Cup. The final replay against Swansea at Ninian Park on 1st May 1915, was the club's final game until after the war.

In contrast to the events of 1914, once war was declared on 3rd September 1939, the Football League programme of 1939-40 was immediately suspended and the government forbade any major sporting events, so that for a while there was no football of any description. Eventually the game was reintroduced and after a number of friendly matches, the game was reorganised into regions. The Robins played in the Regional League (West Division) and though they lost heavily in away games at Manchester City and Manchester United, both teams were beaten 3-2 at the Racecourse. For the rest of the wartime period, Wrexham played in the Regional League (North Division) and in the Second Championship in 1943-44, came second out of 50 clubs. Also during the war years, Wrexham made the most of the 'guest' system with a number of English and Welsh internationals representing the Racecourse Ground club.

WATKIN, STEVE

Local-born striker Steve Watkin played his first game for the Robins at Torquay United in October 1990, and scored his first goal for the club two games later in a 3-2 win at Gillingham. The following season he scored five goals in the club's FA Cup run including a hat-trick in a 5-2 win over non-League Winsford United and a goal in the Robins' 2-1 third round win over Arsenal. In 1992-93 when the club won promotion to the Second Division as runners-up to Cardiff City, Watkin was the leading scorer with 18 League goals in 33 appearances.

A Welsh 'B' international, a feature of his play is his unselfishness in laying on chances for his team-mates whilst he still continues to score his fair share of goals.

There is no doubt that his favourite competition is the FA Cup where he has scored 12 goals in 22 appearances including six as substitute and it was his forward play that helped the club reach the sixth round in 1996-97. He left the Racecourse Ground in 1997-98 to join Swansea City after having scored 76 goals in 258 first team appearances for the Robins.

WATNEY CUP

This was Britain's first commercially sponsored tournament and was a pre-season competition for the top two highest scoring teams in each division of the Football League the previous season. They could only compete if they had no other European involvement.

Wrexham's only match in this competition saw them lose 2-1 at home to West Bromwich Albion on 30th July 1972, with Albert Kinsey scoring the Robins' goal in front of a 11,213 crowd.

WEBBER, KEITH

Though he once took part in a final Welsh Schools rugby trial, Keith Webber joined Everton as a full-time professional and made his League debut against Chelsea on 18th February 1961. However, though he played against Liverpool at Anfield in the Liverpool Senior Cup Final in front of a 54,000 full house, he only managed four first team games in three and a half years at Goodison Park and so in April 1963, he jumped at the chance to join Brighton and Hove Albion for a fee of £17,000. He scored 14 goals in 35 games for the Seagulls but a year later he was surprisingly allowed to leave the Goldstone Ground and join Wrexham for a cut price fee of £4,500.

After making his debut in a 2-0 home defeat by Doncaster Rovers he went on to score 11 goals in 28 games including a spell of nine goals in 11 games. In 1965-66 when Wrexham finished bottom of the Football League, Webber was the club's top scorer with 22 League goals including a hat-trick in a 6-3 home win over Barnsley.

After a fight on the pitch with one of his own team-mates, he was allowed to join Doncaster Rovers for £6,000. The Cardiff-born forward later played for Chester and Stockport County but sadly died at the early age of 40.

WELSH CUP

The Welsh Cup is the third oldest cup competition in the world and was instituted in 1877 with the first final being played at Acton Park, Wrexham on 30th March 1878. Wrexham met the Druids and won

1-0, the man scoring the goal being James Davies, who had helped to form the Welsh FA two years previously. The match was historic for more reasons than one. The style adopted in those days by every team in the country was goalkeeper, two full-backs, two half-backs and six forwards. The Wrexham captain Charles Murless pulled one of his forwards back to form a half-back line of three and so introduced the formation that was to become standard for the next 70 years or so. The other item of note about that first final – the Cup didn't exist – they had no money to buy one!

Wrexham, the oldest surviving club in Wales have appeared in more Welsh Cup Finals (45) than any other team and no side has won the Cup more often than the Robins with 23 wins. They have also held the runners-up position, 22 times.

Below are the years when Wrexham have won the trophy:

1878	Druids	1-0	Acton Park
1883	Druids	1-0	Racecourse Ground
1893	Chirk	2-1	Oswestry
1897	Newtown	2-0	Oswestry
1903	Beramon	8-0	Racecourse Ground
1905	Aberdare	3-0	Racecourse Ground
1909	Chester	1-0	Racecourse Ground
1910	Chester	2-1	Racecourse Ground
1911	Connahs Quay	6-0	Racecourse Ground
1914	Llanelli	3-0*	Oswestry
1915	Swansea Town	1-0	Ninian Park
1921	Pontypridd	3-1*	Shrewsbury
1924	Merthyr Tydfil	1-0*	Racecourse Ground
1925	Flint Town	3-1	Racecourse Ground
1931	Shrewsbury Town	7-0	Racecourse Ground
1957	Swansea Town	2-1	Ninian Park
1958	Chester	2-1*	Racecourse Ground
1960	Cardiff City	1-0*	Racecourse Ground
1972	Cardiff City	3-2**	
1975	Cardiff City	5-2**	
1978	Bangor City	3-1**	
1986	Kidderminster.H.	3-2**	
1995	Cardiff City	2-1	Cardiff Arms Park

* After a replay; ** On aggregate

WELSH LEAGUE

Due to a lack of club funds, Wrexham withdrew from the Combination League and entered the Welsh League for season 1894-95. Wrexham won all eight home matches including an 11-1 rout of Caergwrle to win the championship. Their only defeat came in the opening match of the season when they lost 6-1 at Chirk. In 1895-96, Wrexham again only lost one game in winning the title. At the end of that season, the club returned to the Combination League after discovering they were losing support due to the limited attraction of the opposition in the Welsh League.

WESTON, DON

After representing East Derbyshire Boys, he was spotted by Wrexham while playing for the 31st Training Regiment Royal Artillery (North Wales) and signed in June 1958.

He made his debut in a 1-0 defeat at Swindon Town on the opening day of the 1958-59 season and though he only played in 17 League games, he averaged a goal every other game. Also that season he scored a hat-trick in a 5-1 Welsh Cup victory over Merthyr Tydfil. At the start of the following season, Weston scored in six successive games and ended the campaign as the club's top scorer with 13 goals. In January 1960 he joined Birmingham City for £12,000 but failed to settle at St Andrew's and moved to Rotherham United, where he appeared in the League Cup Final against Aston Villa for the Millmoor club.

In December 1962 he joined Leeds United for £18,000 and made the best possible start to his Elland Road career by scoring a hat-trick on his debut in a 3-1 win against Stoke City. In the Yorkshire club's Second Division championship-winning season of 1963-64 he missed just two games and was the club's top scorer with 18 goals. After three years at Elland Road in which he netted 24 goals in 68 League games, he moved to nearby Huddersfield Town before rejoining Wrexham in December 1966.

He took his total of goals for Wrexham to 49 in 97 games before leaving to play for Chester. He later entered non-League football with Bethesda.

WHITTLE, GRAHAM

Liverpool-born forward Graham Whittle signed professional forms for Wrexham in the summer of 1971 after making his first team debut in a 4-3 win at Aston Villa on 1 May 1971, aged just 17. The following season he established himself as a first team regular and over the next nine seasons proved himself to be a prolific marksman. His best season in terms of goals scored was 1976-77 when he netted 35 goals in 59 League and Cup games, including four in a 6-2 home win over Port Vale and a hat-trick in a 4-2 victory over rivals Chester, also at the Racecourse Ground.

He topped the club's scoring charts again the following season with 18 League goals as the Robins won promotion to the Second Division as champions of the Third Division. He scored all four goals in a 4-1 win at Carlisle United and then netted a hat-trick in the 7-1 thrashing

of Rotherham United which ensured their would be Second Division football at the Racecourse Ground in 1978-79. Also that season he won his third Welsh Cup winners' medal after scoring in the two previous successes against Cardiff City in 1972 and 1975.

Sadly after he had scored 117 goals in 394 first team outings, the career of 28-year-old Graham Whittle was ended when a specialist warned him not to play League football again or risk being crippled in later life. He did play non-League football for a while before turning his hand to coaching.

Graham Whittle

WILLIAMS, ALVAN

After a number of impressive displays for Cheshire League side Staly-
bridge Celtic, Alvan Williams joined Bury but after only two League
appearances for the Shakers he moved to the Racecourse Ground in
the summer of 1956. He made his debut in the opening game of the
1956-57 season in a 2-2 draw at home to Chester but in what turned
out to be his only season at Wrexham, he made just 13 appearances,
scoring seven goals.

He joined Bradford Park Avenue and began to enjoy regular first
team football, scoring 21 goals in 92 games. He later played for Exeter
City before ending his playing career with non-League Bangor City.

In 1964 he was appointed manager of Hartlepool United and in his
only season in charge, they finished 15th in Division Four. He then
took over at Southend United but after they were relegated at the end
of the 1965-66 campaign he lost his job the following season, even
though they were well placed in the League.

Williams was appointed Wrexham manager in April 1967 and appointed future Robins' manager John Neal as his trainer. He also set
up a youth policy which was later to produce a wealth of talent over
the next few years. Wrexham finished eighth in the Fourth Division
in his only full season in charge and in September 1968 he resigned
after a dispute with the directors.

WILLIAMS, MIKE

After failing to make the grade at Everton where he was an apprentice
schoolboy, he joined Chester. Though he had only played in 34
League games for the then Sealand Road club, his performances were
such that a number of top clubs soon took notice. It looked as though
he would be joining John Neal's Chelsea side but he suffered cartilage
trouble and in the summer of 1984 he was rather surprisingly given a
free transfer by the Cestrians.

Wrexham manager Bobby Roberts brought him to the Racecourse
Ground and he made his debut as a substitute for Kevin Rogers
against Swindon Town in the opening match of the 1984-85 season.
Over the next six seasons, Williams was a regular in the Wrexham
side, winning a Welsh Cup winners' medal in 1986 and helping the
club to the Fourth Division play-offs in 1988-89.

Sadly, his career was curtailed by a persistent knee injury and at the age of only 26, Mike Williams, who had played in 238 games for the Robins was forced to retire.

WILLIAMS, TOM

Though he had never played League football, Tom Williams had an eye for spotting talent and scouted for Burnley, Blackburn Rovers and Wrexham. With the outbreak of the Second World War, he became assistant-manager to Tom Morgan at the Racecourse Ground. When Morgan left the club in 1942, he took over as manager and built up a star-studded side with 'guest' players such as Stan Cullis, Jackie Milburn and Johnny Hancocks, so that the Robins were able to compete with the likes of Liverpool.

When the war finished, he had to rebuild the side and in 1947-48 they finished third, although they were ten points adrift of the champions, Lincoln City. Many Wrexham fans felt he was hard done by when asked to resign after a board meeting following an internal dispute. He refused and was sacked.

Williams bought a sports shop in Wrexham and scouted for Liverpool but he remained popular with both players and supporters and his name was often put forward when the manager's job became available. Unfortunately, Tom Williams had enemies on the board of directors and was never appointed.

WORLD WIDE WEB

The address (URL) of the unofficial World Wide Web site for Wrexham is:

http://www.csm.uwe.ac.uk/~khender/wxm/index.html

This is a treasure trove of information for Wrexham supporters with access to the Internet. Both English and Welsh front pages are available.

WORST START

The club's worst-ever start to a season was in 1951-52. It took seven League games to record the first victory of the season as the Robins lost all six of their opening fixtures. The dismal run ended with a 2-1 success over Halifax Town at the Racecourse Ground on 8 September 1951.

WORTHINGTON, GARY

A member of a famous footballing family, his uncle being Frank Worthington, an England international, he began his career as an apprentice with Manchester United. Not being offered professional terms, he joined Huddersfield Town but illness and injuries prevented him from playing first team football. He then signed for Darlington and in 40 League appearances for the Quakers, netted 15 goals before joining Wrexham after the north-east club had lost their League status.

He made his debut for the Robins in the opening game of the 1989-

90 season, scoring Wrexham's goal in a 2-1 defeat at Scarborough. He ended the season as the club's top scorer with 12 League goals, thus ensuring the Robins' League safety. He continued to find the net with great regularity the following season but in March 1991 after scoring 29 goals in 94 games, he left the Racecourse Ground to join Wigan Athletic in exchange for Ian Griffiths. In 1991-92, his first full season at Springfield Park, he was the club's top scorer with 15 goals but after an injury-hit 1992-93 campaign, he was allowed to leave the Latics after scoring 24 goals in 74 League and Cup games. He ten joined Exeter City before ending his League career with Doncaster Rovers.

Gary Worthington

WYNN, RON

Ron Wynn represented Wrexham Schoolboys just before the outbreak of the Second World War and after serving in the Royal Navy during the hostilities joined Chester. However, after only one season at Sealand Road he left to sign for Wrexham o the recommendation of former Aston Villa star, Tommy Gardiner. Wynn joined the Robins as a centre-forward but failed to make much of an impression and was converted to full-back. He made his debut for the club in a 1-1 draw at Barrow in March 1948 and at the end of that season, signed professional forms.

During his nine seasons at the Racecourse Ground, he showed his versatility by playing in eight different positions for the club. During the 1949-50 season he played 17 games at centre-forward and was the club's joint top scorer with nine League goals including a hat-trick in a 3-0 home win over Rochdale.

He went on to play in 190 League and Cup games for the Robins and appeared in 12 Welsh Cup ties, including the final of 1950 when Wrexham lost 4-1 to Swansea Town at Ninian Park.

'X'

In football 'X' traditionally stands for a draw. The club record for the number of draws in a season was in 1966-67 and 1986-87 when on each occasion they managed 20 draws out of 46 matches.

'X' is also the Roman numeral for '10'. Wrexham's highest league score is 10-1 against Hartlepool United. Until recently, it was the only time that a Football League game contained three hat tricks! See also 'Hat-Trick Heroes'.

XMAS DAY

There was a time when football matches were regularly played on Christmas Day but in recent years, the game's authorities have dropped the fixture from their calendar.

The first time Wrexham played on Christmas Day was 1893 when they lost 4-3 at home to Stoke Swifts in the Combination League. During the club's years in the Birmingham and District League, they played the Reserve sides of First Division clubs on Christmas Day in games that produced high scoring affairs. In 1909 they went down 6-0 at Aston Villa and two years later, 6-2 at Wolverhampton Wanderers. In 1914, Wrexham beat Birmingham Reserves 6-2.

The club's first Football League game to be played on Christmas Day saw them play out a goalless draw at Crewe Alexandra. On Christmas Day 1928, the Robins drew 4-4 at Rochdale but had to wait until their eighth League match on this day before winning a game, when they defeated Tranmere Rovers 2-1 in 1933. The club's first eleven Christmas Day fixtures were all played away from the Racecourse Ground and it was 1937 when Wrexham beat Barrow 1-0 before the Robins played a home game on 25 December.

Over the years, Wrexham have suffered some heavy defeats on Christmas Day – and lost three matches by a 5-0 scoreline – Accrington Stanley (1931); Walsall (1935) and Doncaster Rovers (1936).

During the war years, Wrexham played Crewe Alexandra at Gresty Road and went down 8-2 to the Railwaymen.

The last game Wrexham played on Christmas Day was in 1959 when they travelled to Highfield Road and lost 5-3 to Coventry City.

YNYS MÔN REDS

This supporters' club is organised by Gary Pritchard. He can be contacted at 3 Parc Branwen, Y Gorad, Y Fali, Ynys Môn LL65 3AW. Tel: 01407 741574.

YOUNGEST PLAYER

The youngest player to appear in a first-class fixture for Wrexham is Ken Roberts who played in the Third Division (North) match against Bradford Park Avenue (Away 0-5) on 1 September 1951 when he was 15 years 158 days old. He shares the record with Albert Geldard of Bradford Park Avenue as the two youngest players to play in the Football League.

Z

ZENITH

Taking the literal meaning of 'Zenith' as 'high point', few fans will argue over which moment has been the finest in the club's history. In 1977-78, Arfon Griffith's first season as player-manager, the Robins won the Third Division championship and promotion to the Second Division for the first time in their history, which they clinched with a 7-1 win over Rotherham United. The FA Cup saw Wrexham reach the sixth round for only the second time in their history. Sadly, they went down 3-2 to Arsenal with Dixie McNeil who scored in each of the club's nine matches in the competition, netting the club's opening goal. In the Football League Cup, Wrexham reached the fifth round before losing 3-1 at home to Liverpool. For good measure, the Robins won the Welsh Cup to earn themselves a place in the European Cup Winners' Cup for the 1978-79 season.

GOLF COURSES OF NORTH WALES

Visiting Wales and wondering where to play? Maybe you play at a local course and wonder what another course is like. In either case, this is the book you need. Written with authority by Mark Rowlinson and Peter Lees, each course is described in detail and the book is fully illustrated. The only book about the golf courses of North Wales - "Detailed descriptions and advice on how to play the courses are invaluable, as is the assistance of Peter Lees, 30 years a PGA professional." ALL SPORT & LEISURE MONTHLY

£9.95

**COME ON CYMRU!
FOOTBALL IN WALES**

**"Keith Haynes is the
Welsh Nick Hornby** . . .
you won't put this book
down until you've read it
from cover to cover." -
Future magazine.
Includes contributions
from leading Welsh
fanzine writers.
The highs and the lows
of Welsh football,
nationally and
internationally.
An entertaining read -
even for
non-Welsh-football
supporters!
£6.95

All of our books are available through your local bookseller. In case
of difficulty, or for a free catalogue, please contact: **SIGMA LEISURE,
1 SOUTH OAK LANE, WILMSLOW, CHESHIRE S K9 6AR.**

Phone: 01625-531035; Fax: 01625-536800.
E-mail: sigma.press@zetnet.co.uk .
Web site: http://www.sigmapress.co.uk

VISA and MASTERCARD welcome. Please add £2 p&p to all
orders.

We publish a wide range of local interest books covering all of the North West, and throughout most of Britain. Here is a small selection:

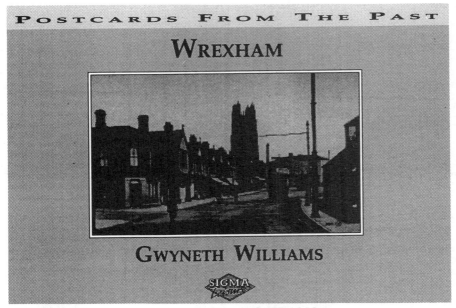

POSTCARDS FROM THE PAST: WREXHAM

Take a lingering look into Wrexham's past with this excellent selection of black and white postcards. The collection gives an insight into the way that the town has developed over the years, whilst evoking nostalgic memories of the old ways of life. Will fascinate residents and those interested in local history.

£6.95